Almost

Ebony L Harris

Faith2FaithBooks

Contents

Preface	1
Onset One: Journey To Almost	5
1 Power and Paranoia	7
2 Transition of Power	9
3 The Fox's Web	11
4 The Persecutor's Throne	13
5 Herod Agrippa the Second (The Last Herod)	17
6 Agrippa's Almost	21
7 Waiting for an Almost	23
8 Don't Settle for Almost	29
Onset Two: Exploring Almost	31
9 Jonah - Almost Emancipated	33
10 Josiah - Almost Heeded	41
11 Elijah - Almost Rejuvenated	45
12 Balaam - Almost Submissive	51
13 David - Almost Ethical	55
14 Solomon - Almost Steadfast	63

15	Laban - Almost Fulfilled	75
16	The Israelites - Almost Believed	79
17	Thief on the Cross - Almost Redeemed	91
18	The Rich Man - Almost Compassionate	95
19	The Rich Young Ruler - Almost Unburdened	101
20	Simon - Almost Humble	109
21	Esau - Almost Satisfied	115
22	Samson - Almost Disciplined	121
23	Gideon - Almost Unwilling	127
24	Simon the Sorcerer - Almost Unchanged	131
25	Gehazi - Almost Aligned	137
26	Eli - Almost Devoted	145
27	Tamar - Almost Mended	153
28	Belshazzar - Almost Prudent	159
29	The Samarian Woman - Almost Hopeful	163
30	Almost Entered In	175
	About The Author	185
	Other Books By This Author	187

Preface

How often do we go about our days making choices without weighing the consequences of our actions? When presented with options, what do you do? We often make decisions only to look back at the times we regret. The best choice you will ever make is to prepare for eternity.

Throughout the New Testament, there is a theme to forsake and follow. It means abandoning other allegiances, distractions, and priorities to follow Christ. It calls for wholehearted devotion and commitment to Jesus as Savior and Lord.

> "So likewise, whosoever he be of you that forsaketh not all that he hath, he cannot be my disciple."
>
> **Luke 14:33**

> "Then said Jesus unto his disciples, 'If any man will come after me, let him deny himself, and take up his cross, and follow me."
>
> **Matthew 16:24**

Whether we invest time or not, we spend our lives preparing for eternity. So the question is, "Are you prepared for eternity? No matter what your answer is, keep reading. In my short existence on this earth, I've discovered that most people have a commitment level that they are willing to uphold. Still, it often varies based on their priorities, values, circumstances, and the "who" or "what" they are committed to.

The next question is: Who or what are you committed to? When making a list in order of the level of your commitment, "who" or "what" do you place at the top? I hope God was at the top of that list. How do you know if He is? Do you prioritize your relationship with God (fasting, praying, devotion, and living for Him) above everything else? Friend, if you must always fit God into your schedule, He isn't a priority. Often, we are pulled in so many directions that our time gets spread thin when it comes to God. How much time will you invest in preparing to meet the bridegroom? Are you willing to pay the price for the anointing that God desires to put on your life?

I initially started researching Acts 26, which quickly spiraled into an in-depth study of the various individuals from the Bible. I pray that this book will help someone see the gravity of their choices. The book of Proverbs speaks of wisdom crying out in the streets to all those who would hear her. Wisdom is always crying out, yet many continue making the wrong choices. That's because wisdom isn't the only thing crying out to us. Our battle is spiritual, and the enemy constantly seeks whom he may devour. He may leave you for a season, but he often returns.

I didn't want to write another devotional but a personal study guide. Consider going through the chapters with a friend as you start this book. It's also great for book clubs. Remember, the Bible is our roadmap to heaven, and it doesn't just show us "a" way to enter in, but "The Only Way" to go. We must constantly examine ourselves. If we are to be counted worthy to obtain everlasting life, we shouldn't be satisfied with "almost" doing the will of God. Take notes, research what you read, and then review it in your Bible.

> "Study to shew thyself approved unto God, a workman that needeth not to be ashamed, rightly dividing the word of truth."
>
> 2 Timothy 2:15

Onset One: Journey to Almost

Within each of us, there is a longing for something more. It is a divine call from our Creator, which leads us to our purpose in Him. Unfortunately, many have settled for a surface-level acquaintance rather than a deeper connection.

We begin our journey to 'almost' with the story of Herod the Great and those who followed after him. We explore their lives and ask questions to help us examine ourselves and what God would have us do. We then focus on the Apostle Paul and his role in the story and how it continues to affect us today. In the last chapter of Onset One, we take an inward gaze as we choose not to settle for living almost in any area of our lives.

"Living 'almost' delivered is not how anyone should live their lives. People of God, we were called for more! We need to muster up our courage and embrace what God has designed for each one of us. Children of the Most High, let us look at the individuals in this book, exploring their lives and rejecting the mindset to settle for an almost attitude when it comes to any part of our lives.

1

Power and Paranoia

King Herod the Great ruled with an iron fist, always hungry for more power. His reign was filled with bloodshed and oppression, casting a dark shadow over the land. But even in these tough times, whispers of hope spread through Judah. These whispers were about the promises God gave through the prophets, written in scrolls so Israel wouldn't forget. They spoke of a promised King, a Messiah who would bring salvation to the people.

Herod the Great was a king who often interacted with the Jewish people. He attended their festivals and built temples, which might make one think he was a believer. However, Herod's actions were largely politically motivated to gain favor with the Jewish population. During that time, powerful individuals who became proselytes were not always required to undergo circumcision, unlike those of lower status. By attending major festivals and making significant contributions, Herod gave the impression that he was devout in the eyes of the people. This can be seen as similar to how some people today might use religious appearances for social or political gain.

He became obsessed with preserving his rule and was consumed by the idea of eliminating this King, which proves that he believed the prophets and was no spectator to the unfolding events but an active participant. Driven by fear and a desperate desire to retain his grasp on authority, he devoted years to pursuing this mysterious persona.

Anticipation filled the room as Herod learned of the King's arrival. He thought he could quietly eliminate this threat without anyone knowing. Yet, he underestimated the God of Israel. His covert plan fell apart, and as panic set in, Herod became desperate. He issued an unthinkable decree to secure his reign—a darkness that would forever haunt Bethlehem. Every innocent male child aged two and under faced a cruel fate. And a cry echoed in Ramah as Rachel wept inconsolably for her lost children. No solace, no comfort could ease her torment. The land trembled under the weight of grieving mothers, mourning the absence of their precious children taken overnight.

The "Massacre of the Innocents" revealed Herod the Great's true intentions, yet the one he pursued, Jesus, evaded his grasp. Following Herod's death, a power struggle unfolded among his successors. Two of his sons emerged, each striving to claim their portion of the fallen king's dominion. Archelaus, the eldest, sought to rule Judea and Samaria, while Herod Antipas, shrewd and calculating, aimed to govern Galilee and Perea. King Agrippa I did not immediately ascend to any territory. Instead, he spent his formative years in Rome, cultivating relationships with Roman emperors. Later, during the reigns of Emperor Caligula and then Emperor Claudius, Herod Agrippa I was granted authority over specific regions.

2

Transition of Power

In times of unrest, it's important to remember that God is in control and has a wise plan for everything. Even when things are uncertain, we can trust that God is watching over His Word and ensures its fulfillment.

In the case of Joseph, the dream he received was a clear message, guiding him to protect and nurture the promised King, Jesus. The transition of power may have had some in the dark about the character of the next king, yet God knew the ambitions and potential dangers lurking under the rule of Archelaus. By leading Joseph to settle in Galilee, He ensured the safety and well-being of His beloved Son. The schemes and manipulations of men never thwart God's plans. Jesus Himself, as the Word made flesh, embodies the fulfillment of God's promises throughout history. All prophecies are completed in Him, and hopes and dreams are realized. Through Jesus, God establishes His kingdom, bringing the opportunity of redemption to a world torn apart by sin.

We can find hope in knowing God is in control. He watches over His Word (as he watched over Jesus), ensuring its fulfillment in the perfect time and manner. As we reflect on the events surrounding Jesus as a child, we are reminded of God's faithfulness. With a God so invested in His investments, we know we can lean and depend on Him, even when the path seems uncertain.

> **"Now unto him that is able to keep you from falling, and to present you faultless before the presence of his glory with exceeding joy, To the only wise God our Saviour, be glory and majesty, dominion and power, both now and ever. Amen."**
>
> **Jude verses 24 and 25**

I know we are talking about the journey to Almost, but I must briefly pause to tell you that you can trust God. We aren't talking about a man but God, the Creator, who knows everything we are going through and will go through. Remember that He knows the end from the beginning when we can't make sense of things.

3

The Fox's Web

Herod Antipas often surveyed his kingdom, having a calculating eye. Behind his charming facade lay a heart steeped in disloyalty, always scheming to protect his power and preserve his reign. He, too, heard whispers of Jesus, not as a child to be born but as a man who walked the earth.

During the earthly ministry of Jesus, some Pharisees warned Him about Herod's intention to kill Him. But Jesus saw through the veils of deception. He compared him to a cunning fox, a symbol of cleverness and manipulation. Jesus knew that Herod Antipas, like the fox, would use his wiles to exploit the situation for his advantage, seeking to trap what he hoped to be an unsuspecting Messiah and safeguard his position.

As Herod Antipas sat in his court, anticipation coursed through his veins. Reports of this Jesus had reached his ears. Tales of miraculous healings and profound teachings that had ignited the people's hearts. Could this be the long-awaited Messiah the promised King his father searched for, delivered right into his hands?

> "At that time, some Pharisees came to Jesus and said to him, 'Leave this place and go somewhere else. Herod wants to kill you.' He replied, 'Go tell that fox, 'I will keep on driving out demons and healing people today and tomorrow, and on the third day I will reach my goal.' In any case, I must press on today and tomorrow and the next day—for surely no prophet can die outside Jerusalem!"
>
> Luke 13:31-33

As the appointment drew near, it brought Herod face to face with the King, who he believed challenged his existence. This Herod sought Jesus during his ministry, not out of repentance but driven by something dark.

Yet, an unexpected emptiness swept over the ruler as the Messiah finally stood before him. The displays of power he had envisioned remained elusive, along with the signs he had craved that failed to manifest. Jesus, in that moment of reckoning, shattered all Herod's expectations. Surely, this wasn't the "King of the Jews!"

The truth of Jesus slipped through his fingers. The only Herod to see Him couldn't even recognize Him. After a while, His disciples didn't recognize Him. Although He said it repeatedly, no one expected Jesus, who had the opportunity and the power to defend Himself, to accept such a shameful death. Most would attempt to avoid it at any cost.

4

The Persecutor's Throne

With an intelligent mind and eloquent tongue, Herod Agrippa, the first, forged alliances and manipulated circumstances to ascend the ladder of power. Like his father, he also kept the Jewish festivals. But as Agrippa's thirst for power grew, so did his disdain for those who stood in his way. With his inherited paranoia, he saw potential threats lurking in every corner, and he would not tolerate any challenge to his authority. It was in this power-hungry climate that the Apostle James found himself entangled.

James, a pillar of the early Church, dared to proclaim the truth of Jesus Christ as the long-awaited Messiah and Son of God. He fearlessly challenged the established order, declaring that salvation and eternal life could be found only through faith in Jesus, not through adherence to religious rituals or the authority of earthly rulers.

Herod Agrippa saw an opportunity to assert dominance over the growing Christian movement. Setting his sights on James, he intended to make him an example. The Apostle James was condemned to death, becoming the first of the Twelve to lay down his life for his faith just fourteen years after the ascension. The news had a reverse effect, igniting a fire of resilience and resolve that would burn for generations.

Not long after the death of the Apostle James, Herod Agrippa, with blood on his hands, made his mark on history. Now, basking in the satisfaction of his perceived victory, he, adorned in royal garments, took his place before a crowd gathered to celebrate a grand occasion. As he was celebrating his greatness, the people marveled at his speech. "The voice of a God and not a man," they declared. A sudden and excruciating pain gripped his abdomen, causing him to double over in agony as word spread that an angel of the Lord had struck down Herod. The once-proud ruler, who had relished in his earthly authority, now found himself at the mercy of a power greater than his own.

> "And upon a set day Herod, arrayed in royal apparel, sat upon his throne, and made an oration unto them. And the people gave a shout, saying, It is the voice of a god, and not of a man. And immediately the angel of the Lord smote him, because he gave not God the glory: and he was eaten of worms, and gave up the ghost."
>
> **Acts 12:21-23**

Despite the best efforts of his physicians, Herod's condition deteriorated rapidly. The whispers of divine justice got louder as the people witnessed the downfall of the man who had dared to take the glory that belonged to God.

In his final moments, Herod Agrippa, consumed by pain and tormented by his past actions, couldn't be helped by the power he attained. The once-mighty ruler, who had stood over the trial of James with a heart devoid of compassion, now faced his mortality with a heavy burden.

After Herod Agrippa's demise, the accounts of his death were not confined to the whispers and beliefs of the early Christian community alone. Both Jewish and Roman historians chronicled the events surrounding the downfall of this ambitious ruler, shedding light on the dramatic turn of fate that befell him.

According to Jewish historian Josephus, Herod Agrippa's sudden demise was attributed to divine retribution. They recounted that during a celebration, as Herod stood before a gathered crowd, an intense pain seized his body. Despite the best efforts of his physicians, his condition worsened, leading to his untimely death. Jewish sources spoke of an angel of the Lord striking him down.

On the other hand, Roman historians approached Herod Agrippa's death differently. They viewed it as a tragic turn of events without divine intervention. According to their accounts, Herod's condition was described as a severe illness, likely acute abdominal distress. They recorded the rapid deterioration of his health over five days, marked by excruciating pain and a rapid decline.

It's important to note that Herod Agrippa was not the first king over captive Israel to be judged by God. Do you remember Nebuchadnezzar? God caused him to be a beast and roam in the wilderness for seven years.

In Daniel chapter 3, Nebuchadnezzar builds a golden statue and commands everyone to bow down and worship it. Shadrach, Meshach, and Abednego, three Jewish officials in Nebuchadnezzar's court, refuse to worship the statue, as it goes against their faith in God. When Nebuchadnezzar learns about their defiance, he confronts them and threatens to throw them into a blazing furnace.

In their response to King Nebuchadnezzar, the young men make it clear that they will not worship the statue, regardless of the consequences. They express their trust in God, saying that they will still not worship the king's statue even if God does not save them from the furnace. Their faith in God was unwavering.

This event leads to Nebuchadnezzar's astonishment when he witnesses God's intervention. His captors are thrown into the fiery furnace but are miraculously protected by God. When Nebuchadnezzar sees this, he acknowledges the power and supremacy of the God of Shadrach, Meshach, and Abednego and praises God.

Years later, this king who once praised and believed God has pride issues, and the God he Praised humbled him for seven years until he humbled himself. Herod, too, once praised and acknowledged God. He was known as a proselyte, and after he and his wife were converted, their son was born a Jew. So, in Herod Agrippa's case, God humbles him for five days instead of seven years. God's spirit will not always strive with man. It was Herod's stomach that was hurting, not his mouth. If Herod believed the prophets, as Paul did, don't you think God would have forgiven him for what he did to His people had he repented? Remember, God is not unrighteous. Time and chance happen to them all. We never know how long we have; life is too short to live an almost repentant life.

5

Herod Agrippa the Second (The Last Herod)

The final Herod, Agrippa the second, was at a critical juncture. From his early years, he had been surrounded by the whispers of the prophets, their words intertwined with the very fabric of his family's history. The Herods before him, including his father, believed in the prophecies, embracing the coming of a future king who would remove them from power. Now, as this Agrippa stood in the presence of the Apostle Paul, the weight of those prophecies bore down upon him. He, too, had a choice to make.

Standing in the presence of King Agrippa, Festus, and Bernice was Paul, as he wrote in his epistles, the prisoner of the Lord. One might say that this was a divine appointment.

Paul:

> "I think myself happy, King Agrippa because today I shall answer for myself before you concerning all the things of which I am accused by the Jews, especially because you are expert in all customs and questions which have to do with the Jews. Therefore I beg you to hear me patiently."
>
> Acts 26: 2-3

As Paul continued, he recounted his strict upbringing as a Pharisee and his zealous persecution of Christians. He emphasized that his encounter with Jesus on the road to Damascus had transformed him from a persecutor into a faithful follower.

Paul:

> "At midday, O king, I saw in the way a light from heaven, above the brightness of the sun, shining round about me and them which journeyed with me. And when we were all fallen to the earth, I heard a voice speaking unto me, and saying in the Hebrew tongue, Saul, Saul, why persecutest thou me? it is hard for thee to kick against the pricks. And I said, Who art thou, Lord? And he said, I am Jesus whom thou persecutest."
>
> Acts 26:13-15

He explained how Jesus appointed him a minister and witness to Jews and Gentiles, delivering them from darkness to light. Paul's words struck a chord with King Agrippa, who was familiar with the rise of the Christian movement and the testimonies of other followers of Jesus.

It was as if Agrippa couldn't help but say what was on his mind:

> "Almost thou persuadest me to be a Christian."
>
> Acts 26:28

Paul, passionately and sincerely, responded:

> "I would to God, that not only thou, but also all that hear me this day, were both almost, and altogether such as I am, except these bonds."
>
> Acts 26:29

The tension in the room grew as Festus, attempting to make sense of Paul's fervent words, interrupted, suggesting that Paul had gone mad due to his extensive learning. Paul, maintaining his composure, addressed Festus:

> "I am not mad, most noble Festus; but speak forth the words of truth and soberness. For the king knoweth of these things, before whom also I speak freely: for I am persuaded that none of these things are hidden from him; for this thing was not done in a corner."
>
> Acts 26:24-26

The events that brought us to this 26th chapter of the Book of Acts were no secret. In this particular statement, Paul is saying that the events and teachings of Jesus, including His life, death, and resurrection, were not hidden or done secretly. These events had a significant public impact and were widely known and witnessed by many.

I know they want us to keep Jesus to ourselves, but the gospel transforms, and it can't be confined to a small group or limited to an upper-room experience. These teachings will go to the ends of the earth.

As Paul is standing in the presence of royalty, he emphasizes the credibility and significance of this message he proclaimed. It was not based on rumors but on tangible events that had a public impact and were widely known. In addition, Jewish and Roman historians speak of spies scattered throughout the region, keeping a watchful eye on the activities of these believers. The news of Jesus' death and resurrection had spread, and the movement of His followers was steadily growing.

Recognizing Paul's innocence, Festus turned to King Agrippa, explaining that the accusations against Paul lacked any substantial evidence. He revealed the widespread outcry among the Jews in Jerusalem and Cecerea, demanding Paul's execution. However, upon examining the case, Festus found no grounds for a death sentence. Since Paul appealed to Caesar, Festus sent him to Rome.

6

Agrippa's Almost

As Paul stood before Agrippa, his voice sounded with unwavering conviction. It was not a plea for release that escaped Paul's lips but a heartfelt cry for the very soul of a king. Within his words, Paul, the chosen vessel, held a transformative power capable of shattering the chains that bound King Agrippa's heart.

Agrippa, adorned with vast knowledge and enriched experiences, found himself confronted with the truth he had spent his life looking for. However, the question remained: would he embrace it, surrendering his entire life to the call of God? Or would he settle for an "almost," a superficial proximity to God that offered no genuine redemption?

Friend, as we journey through time, let us never forget that God will go to great lengths for a soul. His reach extends into the depths of human existence; His hand outstretched even to those entangled in the web of darkness. Agrippa's story reminds us that the kingdom of heaven remains within our grasp regardless of the depths of our sins.

So, let us resist the temptation to settle for a life filled with "almost." Refuse to be content with living within the proximity of God. Instead, strive to make it in. When we enter into eternity, no room exists for half-hearted efforts or lukewarm, almost Christians.

Now is the time to consider: What is your "almost"? What stands between you and embracing the fullness of God's grace? We can see how far God was willing to go for King Agrippa. With so many family members pursuing the Messiah for the wrong rationales, Agrippa was sought for all the right reasons. I pray that you embrace the truth, surrendering your life to the One who pursues you, longing for your heart to be wholly His.

7

Waiting for an Almost

Paul's journey and imprisonment also remind us not to settle for "almost" fulfilling the work of the Lord. As he traveled from Miletus to various cities, warnings echoed in his ears. There were multiple cautionary messages in Caesarea, and the prophet Agabus even enacted a prophetic sign of his impending arrest and imprisonment. Friends and companions urged him to reconsider his plans, fearing for his safety. But Paul, guided by the Holy Spirit, remained steadfast.

He was eventually taken into custody, yet words of encouragement and direction echoed in his heart:

> "Take courage, for as you have testified to the facts about me in Jerusalem, so you must testify also in Rome."
>
> Acts 23:11

These words reminded him that his trials and imprisonment were not in vain.

Paul encountered numerous opportunities during captivity to demonstrate his commitment to the Lord. His path took a new turn when a conspiracy formed to take his life. He would be escorted to Caesarea, where he would be imprisoned for safety.

Paul had multiple encounters with Roman governors Felix and Festus, fearlessly proclaiming his innocence and boldly sharing the gospel. Despite their desire for him to secure his freedom through bribes or compromise, he refused to give in to such measures, understanding that a life lived for God's purpose cannot be bought or sold. Instead, he patiently endured, trusting in God's timing and plan.

His imprisonment continued in Rome but did not deter him from the mission. He penned powerful letters in his affliction to various churches, including the books of Colossians, Philemon, Ephesians, and Philippians. These prison epistles are rich with wisdom and guidance, reflecting Paul's faith and the lessons he learned through his trials.

In his affliction, he writes:

"Endeavouring to keep the unity of the Spirit in the bond of peace."

Ephesians 4:3

He also says:

"Let all bitterness, and wrath, and anger, and clamour, and evil speaking, be put away from you, with all malice: And be ye kind one to another, tenderhearted, forgiving one another, even as God for Christ's sake hath forgiven you."

Ephesians 4:31-32

In the sixth chapter of Ephesians, he admonishes us,

"Put on the whole armour of God, that ye may be able to stand against the wiles of the devil."

Ephesians 6:11

He encourages us,

"Being confident of this very thing, that he which hath begun a good work in you will perform it until the day of Jesus Christ:"

Philippians 1:6

Paul, was able to encourage us by saying:

> "Do all things without murmurings and disputings:"
>
> Philippians 2:14

He talks about this sweet communion that he and many others partook in saying:

> "That I may know him, and the power of his resurrection, and the fellowship of his sufferings, being made conformable unto his death; If by any means I might attain unto the resurrection of the dead."
>
> Philippians 3:10-11

Don't you want to be counted worthy? I'll ask you again: Are you willing to pay the price for the anointing God has for your life? Paul's imprisonment taught him that an "almost" life falls short of God's intended purpose. He refused to settle for a life of convenience, comfort, or compromise. Instead, he embraced the challenges and trials, knowing they were part of a greater plan. From his time in captivity, he emerged with a greater understanding of God's sovereignty, the power of faith, and the necessity of spiritual armor.

These examples teach us the value of embracing God's calling despite trials and opposition. We are reminded not to settle for almost. Consider it: Paul's letters help us today in our faith. What if he decided almost to do the will of God? How different would our lives be if he had almost written those epistles? Prisons back then were not what they are today. It's not like he was in comfort. His resolve way back then has strengthened many today.

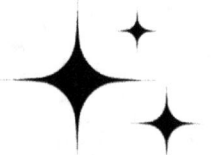

8

Don't Settle for Almost

Imagine, if you will, a life where "almost" becomes the norm. How many of us have fallen victim to this word? We come close to reaching our goals and tasting victory, yet we allow many opportunities to slip through our fingers. But why? Why do we settle for almost when we have the potential to achieve so much more?

What if we refuse to settle for almost? What if we challenge ourselves to break free from the limitations that almost impose? Overcoming almost lies in our choice—to either accept almost or rise above it.

Imagine a life where "almost" becomes a thing of the past, where we seize every opportunity, fully commit to God, and live unashamed of our faith. A life where we witness, forgive, and break generational curses—a life of deliverance, healing, and sanctification. The power to deny the flesh, to rise early for prayer, and to truly live an abundant life in God. My friends, the world waits for us to shed the cloak of almost and embrace our true potential. We are not destined for an almost salvation or an almost life. We are destined for greatness, victory, and a resounding 'Well done' from our Creator. So, I implore you not to settle for almost. Together, let us make a lasting impact on this world. When the Lord cracks the sky, we don't want to be among those who almost made it in.

Onset Two: Exploring Almost

In this section, we examine the lives of figures from the Bible. Their stories speak to us from the past, shedding light on missed opportunities and untaken paths. Looking at their lives, we are confronted with the reality that we, too, have stood on the brink of "almost." These case studies are an invitation for introspection, self-examination, and transformation. We are challenged to confront unhealthy patterns, identify potential opportunities that may be slipping away, and make the necessary changes to live wholly for God.

Each turn of the page propels us forward with a sense of urgency as we uncover lessons and wisdom that can guide us through uncertain times. This book sheds light on the paths we should take. I also pray that you gain insight from the case studies and gather the strength and determination to confront your missed opportunities and break free from the limitations of "almost" fulfilling the will of God in your life.

9

Jonah - Almost Emancipated

God chose a prophet to preach that destruction would surely come to Nineveh. Jonah was a gifted preacher, yet within his heart, prejudice lurked, clouding his judgment and distorting his perception of these people notorious for their cruelty and inhumane treatment of their enemies. Their acts of violence and torture left scars on the hearts of those who suffered or had relatives who suffered at their hands. It's very likely that Jonah either directly or indirectly witnessed the pain and suffering inflicted upon his people, which fueled this deep resentment and desire for their destruction.

When God called him to go to Nineveh and warn the city of impending doom, he ran. The thought of extending mercy to a people he believed was undeserving of it gnawed at his soul. Jonah longed for their demise, hoping they would face the full wrath of God's judgment. If we are not careful, things can happen in life, and we can pass judgment on people who have hurt us or our family. The hatred we hold on to can make us feel like the offender or individuals related to them are beyond mercy.

Instead of embracing the call, Jonah boards a ship headed in the opposite direction, seeking to hide as if he could escape from God. The Lord sent a violent storm threatening to consume the vessel. Jonah, realizing that his disobedience had brought calamity upon the innocent sailors onboard, willingly threw himself into the raging sea, sacrificing his own life to save them.

However, God's mercy prevailed even in Jonah's disobedience. He sent a great fish to swallow him, preserving his life and granting him a second chance to fulfill his assignment. Reluctantly, Jonah traveled to Nineveh, his heart still heavy with prejudice and resentment.

After walking nonstop through the city, proclaiming that God would destroy it, Jonah retreated to a hill overlooking the town, waiting for its destruction. To His astonishment, the people of Nineveh responded to his message. They repented and turned away from their wickedness, seeking forgiveness from the God they had previously disregarded. But instead of rejoicing at their transformation, Jonah's heart was filled with anger and bitterness. He resented God's mercy toward a people he believed deserved only punishment.

Later, God caused a plant to grow and provide shade for Jonah, giving comfort and relief from the sun. Yet, when God allowed the plant to wither, Jonah became consumed by his grief and anger, lamenting the loss of a mere plant while disregarding the redemption and transformation that had taken place within an entire city.

The Parable of the Unforgiving Servant

This story reminds me of the parable that Jesus told about the unforgiving servant, who would not forgive someone charged with owing him money when he had just received forgiveness from his master for owing far more. He and his whole family were sold into captivity.

I often wondered why this entire family would suffer because of someone else's unforgiveness. At the time of this Parable, poor families would be sold into slavery to pay debts. While it seems unlikely for entire families to be sold into slavery today in America, consider this scenario: You witness a family member being wronged, and because you love them, you develop a hate for the individual who wronged them. Now, the person did no wrong to you, but you willingly hate them for what they did to the person you love. Another scenario would be that you are listening to your friend talk about how an individual wronged them. It didn't happen to you, but you are now upset with the person being talked about, and you harbor it in your heart against them. In both cases, you willingly took on a debt that didn't belong to you. Thus, now you share in the repayment of it.

> "A man void of understanding striketh hands, and becometh surety in the presence of his friend."
>
> **Proverbs 17:8**

In this verse, we are warned about taking on someone else's debt as if it were our own. Many co-sign on issues they have yet to get involved with. Free yourself, forgive, don't get entangled with affairs that don't belong to you.

Let's take a look at what had to be paid. This family was delivered to the tormentors. Friend, don't you know unforgiveness has tormentors? Let me help you identify them. They are those thoughts that keep replaying in your mind. Remember, thoughts are spirits. First, there may be only a few here and there. When you leave them unchecked, they start coming a little more frequently. The thoughts continue until the spirits are so loud it's hard to hear the voice of reason. Someone said, "Don't let the devil ride." Forgive.

In this tale of missed opportunities, Jonah's story is a reminder of the dangers of prejudice and unforgiveness. Despite his gift of preaching and his intimate knowledge of God's mercy, Jonah allowed his biases to overshadow the truth. He clung to a hatred that did not rightfully belong to him, willingly imprisoning himself within the walls of resentment. Jonah lived an almost emancipated life.

Likewise, we are often tempted to hold onto grudges and grievances, allowing the actions of others to dictate our own emotions and attitudes. We sell ourselves into the bondage of unforgiveness, refusing to extend the same mercy and grace freely given to us. But the path to freedom lies in forgiveness. It is an act of liberation, releasing the chains of resentment and allowing healing. Just as forgiveness was bestowed upon us without cost, so should we offer it to others, even in the face of pain and injustice.

In the words of Jesus, a truth is revealed, heavy with consequences. He warns us,

> "Therefore if you bring your gift to the altar, and there remember that your brother has something against you, leave your gift there before the altar, and go your way. First be reconciled to your brother, and then come and offer your gift."
>
> Matthew 5:23-24

Imagine the scene, a moment of worship, an offering ready to be presented. But as you go to offer your worship before the Lord, a memory emerges, a lingering grudge, a broken relationship. Jesus demands our attention, urging us to set aside the very act of worship and prioritize reconciliation.

Let's consider the consequences of ignoring God's instructions. What if we harbor unforgiveness and allow it to fester? It is like we've poisoned our hearts and damaged our relationship with God. The results would be a self-built barrier between us and the fullness of God.

Yet, there is hope within this warning. Jesus beckons us to be reconciled, mend broken bonds, extend, and seek forgiveness. In that act of humility and vulnerability, the chains of unforgiveness can be broken, and the way to true worship is paved.

One thing that holds many back from forgiveness is "the great what if." What if our brother or sister refuses to receive us? The Bible echoes with wisdom, guiding our steps even in the face of rejection.

Jesus Himself teaches us:

> "Moreover if thy brother shall trespass against thee, go and tell him his fault between thee and him alone: if he shall hear thee, thou hast gained thy brother."
>
> Matthew 18:15

We are compelled to initiate this crucial conversation, braving the vulnerability and discomfort that accompany it. But what if, against all our hopes, our brother's heart remains hardened? What if they turn a deaf ear to our plea for forgiveness? Jesus provides further instructions, declaring:

> "But if he will not hear thee, then take with thee one or two more, that in the mouth of two or three witnesses, every word may be established."
>
> Matthew 18:16

We gather trusted witnesses who can testify to the authenticity of our intentions and the situation's gravity. We don't want individuals to take our side but those who would stand on God's side. As we approach our brother once more, we pray that the presence of these witnesses will soften their hearts and lead to reconciliation. Again, getting unbiased individuals and people who will stand for righteousness is vital.

What if even this step fails to yield the desired outcome? Jesus provides further instruction, which states:

> "And if he shall neglect to hear them, tell it unto the church: but if he neglect to hear the church, let him be unto thee as a heathen man and a publican."
>
> Matthew 18:17

This verse presents a challenge, raising questions about how we should respond when our brother refuses to hear us and seek to distance themselves from reconciliation.

Rightly dividing the Word of Truth is critical, especially regarding this verse. Understanding the context and heart of God is crucial. The reference to treating someone as a heathen and a publican does not imply ex-communication or rejection of the individual. Let me reason with you if your first thought is to isolate someone holding on to unforgiveness. Many who are struggling to forgive are hurting. We don't throw wounded Christians to the enemy. That's the equivalent of leaving a bleeding lamb to fend for itself. If not tended to, it won't be long before the devourer comes to retrieve them. Instead, we adopt a change in our approach, reflecting the need for renewed efforts to share the love of God with them. Why? Because, at this time, they don't know the Lord as they should?

As followers of Christ, our calling is to walk out the teachings of Jesus and show compassion to those who are lost. When doctors prescribe medication that doesn't do the intended job, they either increase or decrease the dosage or try something new. When people strive to live for God, if they have an issue with doing things according to God's will, the solution is always the same. That solution is more of Jesus. That means more fasting, praying, reading, and meditating on the Word of God. Just as Jesus engaged with tax collectors and sinners, we are encouraged to reach out to those who have distanced themselves, demonstrating Christ's love and extending the invitation to experience Him on a deeper level. It is, after all, the love of God that leads us to repentance. God's love is the last thing you want to withhold from anyone.

In this scenario, the Scripture urges us to approach our brothers to guide them back to the truth, reminding them of the hope in Jesus. We are to persistently pray for their hearts to be softened and for reconciliation to occur.

Therefore, rather than dismissing or abandoning our brother or sister, we are called to remain open to the possibility of their restoration. The command to treat them as heathen and a publican reminds us of our responsibility to continue showing them the love of Christ, sharing the Gospel, and praying for their spiritual revival. By extending forgiveness, offering prayer, and showing the love of God, we can create an atmosphere conducive to the work of the Holy Spirit, leading to the transformation of their hearts and a restoration of the relationship.

We also recognize that forgiveness and reconciliation are not always within our control. We have fulfilled our responsibility, following the biblical steps earnestly and sincerely. Yet, the outcome rests in the hands of our brother and their willingness to receive and extend forgiveness.

Let Jonah's story serve as a call to examine our hearts. We don't have to live an almost emancipated life. Emancipation awaits those willing to let go of the shackles of hatred and walk in the freedom of forgiveness.

10

Josiah - Almost Heeded

In the land of Judah, a young king ascended to the throne. He was just eight years old when he took the mantle of leadership, inheriting a kingdom plagued by idolatry and spiritual decay. Josiah, however, had a heart that yearned for righteousness and sought to restore true worship to the land.

As the king grew in wisdom and understanding, he became increasingly aware of the waywardness of his people. He witnessed the blatant disregard for God's commandments, the worship of false gods, and the desecration of the sacred temple. Filled with righteous indignation, Josiah knew that drastic measures needed to be taken to bring about spiritual revival.

Driven by a sincere desire to restore the worship of the one true God, Josiah embarked on a mission to purify the land. He ordered the destruction of idols, the tearing down of altars, and the removal of all traces of pagan worship. The people responded to his decree, and the nation transformed spiritually. While cleansing the temple, a copy of the Book of the Law was found. It contained instructions and commandments given by God to His people. Josiah, eager to understand the words of God, commanded that the book be read aloud to him.

As the words of the Law were read, the king's heart was filled with mixed emotions. He realized the depth of his people's disobedience and understood the severity of God's judgment that awaited them. Overwhelmed by a desire to seek God's favor, Josiah reinstated the celebration of Passover, this time as a national observance.

> "Never had a Passover like this been celebrated in Israel during the time of the prophet Samuel or the kings of Israel. They did not celebrate the Passover as Josiah celebrated it with priests, Levites, all of Judah, the people of Israel who could be found, and the inhabitants of Jerusalem. This Passover was celebrated in the eighteenth year of Josiah's reign."
>
> 2 Chronicles 35:18-19

Yes, God was with Josiah, and He used him to do beautiful things, but often, after we are used by the Most High, the enemy attempts to destroy us. Josiah, a righteous king of Judah, faced a critical moment when he was on the verge of disregarding a warning from the Lord. Despite being a devout ruler, he was about to make a decision that would have dire consequences.

At the time, Pharaoh Necho of Egypt was passing through the region, and Josiah felt compelled to confront him in battle. However, Necho sent a message to Josiah, warning him not to interfere and advising him to step aside.

> "But he sent ambassadors to him, saying, What have I to do with thee, thou king of Judah? I come not against thee this day, but against the house wherewith I have war: for God commanded me to make haste: forbear thee from meddling with God, who is with me, that he destroy thee not. Nevertheless, Josiah would not turn his face from him, but disguised himself, that he might fight with him, and hearkened not unto the words of Necho from the mouth of God, and came to fight in the valley of Megiddo."
>
> 2 Chronicles 35:21-22

The message was a clear and direct warning from the Lord, given through Pharaoh Necho. Yet, Josiah's eagerness, sense of duty, or even pride drove him to dismiss the message. Ignoring the divine caution, he pressed forward with his plan to engage in battle against the pharaoh and his forces. Almost heeding the warning of the Lord, and tragically, his decision proved disastrous. An archer fatally wounded him during the war, and he ultimately succumbed to his injuries. The nation mourned the loss of their king, realizing the consequences of his disobedience to the warning of the Lord.

This case study serves as a sobering reminder that even the most devout individuals can make misguided choices when they fail to heed God's warnings. When examining Josiah's life, we see the importance of listening to and obeying God's guidance and cautions, even if they come in unexpected ways or from unexpected sources. God was with Josiah, but God was also with Pharaoh Necho and his forces. No one has a monopoly on God. He is, after all, "Our" Father.

> "But be ye doers of the word, and not hearers only, deceiving your own selves."
>
> James 1:22

Let's look at the consequences of Josiah's lapse in judgment and how it may have influenced the people around him to follow the evil he did. Though it may not have been explicitly written in the commandments, it was still something God required of him. This lapse in judgment was a breach of his covenant with God, a covenant that the people had witnessed and revered. The people had seen Josiah's commitment to following God's commandments. They witnessed his humility in seeking the Lord's guidance before making decisions. But Josiah faltered when he failed to inquire of the Lord and made a decision contrary to God's will; it sent a powerful message to the people.

How does this apply to us today? Josiah lived in a way that when he died, everyone in his kingdom was touched; they recounted how he was a king who followed God with all his heart because they couldn't see his heart. Friend, people may sing your praises, but what does God say? Do your actions align with the good people say about you? We must strive to maintain our commitment to God's commandments, seek His guidance in all decisions, and remain vigilant in our pursuit of righteousness. Doing so can avoid the pitfalls of almost heeding the Lord's commands.

11

Elijah - Almost Rejuvenated

In the aftermath of his victory on Mount Carmel, Elijah found himself physically and emotionally exhausted. When reading on paper, it can be hard to see the magnitude of his challenge and the intensity of the spiritual battle that had drained him to the core. While God used him to achieve a remarkable triumph, he had neglected to find solace and rest in God's provision.

> "Then Jezebel sent a messenger unto Elijah, saying, So let the gods do to me, and more also, if I make not thy life as the life of one of them by to morrow about this time. And when he saw that, he arose, and went for his life, and came to Beersheba, which belongeth to Judah, and left his servant there."
>
> 1 Kings 19:2-3

Elijah's missed opportunity lay in his failure, for a time, to recognize the importance of spiritual rejuvenation. Instead of seeking refuge in God, he succumbed to fear and allowed discouragement to grip his heart. He fled to the wilderness, isolated and burdened by the weight of his calling.

In reviewing this moment, we are reminded of the implications of burnout in our lives. Many of us experience seasons of exhaustion, where the demands of life and the battles we face leave us spiritually depleted. During these times, we must not neglect the invitation to return to our Shepherd, God, the source of everything.

> "The LORD is my shepherd; I shall not want. He maketh me to lie down in green pastures: he leadeth me beside the still waters. He restoreth my soul: he leadeth me in the paths of righteousness for his name's sake. Yea, though I walk through the valley of the shadow of death, I will fear no evil: for thou art with me; thy rod and thy staff they comfort me. Thou preparest a table before me in the presence of mine enemies: thou anointest my head with oil; my cup runneth over. Surely goodness and mercy shall follow me all the days of my life: and I will dwell in the house of the LORD forever."
>
> Psalm 23

Just as Elijah found himself almost rejuvenated, we, too, can be spiritually depleted. We find renewal and restoration when we return to Him. The key lies in recognizing our need for God's presence and seeking Him earnestly. He longs to restore our weary souls and replenish our strength. When we are willing to turn back to Him, we will discover Him waiting to embrace us.

Battling the enemy, whether external or internal, takes a toll on us. The pursuit of living a life pleasing to God and the pressures of everyday life can leave us feeling drained and empty if we attempt to walk in our strength. Let us take advantage of the crucial moment to return to the source, to reconnect with our Creator and sustainer.

> "And he said unto them, Come ye yourselves apart into a desert place, and rest a while: for there were many coming and going, and they had no leisure so much as to eat."
>
> **Mark 6:31**

There was a moment in the life of Jesus and His disciples after they had been actively involved in ministry, teaching, and performing miracles when they were also almost rejuvenated. They had been very busy with people coming and going to see and hear them.

Jesus saw the toll their constant work and interaction with the crowd had taken on them. He suggests that they "come apart into a desert place" or, in some translations, "a quiet place" or "a solitary place." He advises them to take a break, to find a quiet and secluded spot away from the crowds, where they can rest and rejuvenate.

The verse highlights the importance of rest and self-care, even for those ministering to souls. Jesus understood that rest and refreshment were necessary for physical and spiritual well-being. It's a reminder that everyone, including those engaged in ministry, needs moments of solitude and relaxation to recharge and maintain effectiveness.

> "And he [Jesus] withdrew himself into the wilderness, and prayed."
>
> **Luke 5:16**

Often, Jesus Himself would get away from the crowd to reconnect with God.

> "Remember the sabbath day, to keep it holy. Six days shalt thou labour, and do all thy work: But the seventh day is the sabbath of the Lord thy God: in it thou shalt not do any work..."
>
> **Exodus 20:8-10**

Rest is so important that God commanded a day for it. One day out of every seven is set aside as a day of rest, emphasizing the importance of periodic rest and rejuvenation. Even the land was to rest every seventh year.

> "But in the seventh year shall be a sabbath of rest unto the land, a sabbath for the Lord: thou shalt neither sow thy field, nor prune thy vineyard."
>
> **Leviticus 25:4**

While these passages highlight rest on a larger scale (weekly and yearly), they convey the importance of periodic rest as part of God's design for human well-being and the proper use of time.

During the times of Elijah, the people were in a state of moral decay, and they desperately needed someone to give them the Word of God, yet, in serving the people, the servant should always take time to get rejuvenated. It is by returning to the source that we can help others. The need for rest isn't just for those serving God's people. It is for all.

Rest is a physical necessity and a vital component of overall well-being for everyone. Neglecting proper rest can significantly affect physical and mental health, leading to fatigue, stress, and burnout. Also, inadequate rest can take a toll on our emotional well-being, making us more irritable and anxious, making it challenging to provide the emotional support and care that our loved ones and those in need require.

Beyond the physical and emotional aspects, rest also plays a critical role in our spiritual vitality. When we fail to prioritize rest, our spiritual life may suffer, impacting our prayer, meditation, and relationship with God. Lack of rest can also affect how we perceive and navigate our challenges and experiences. It's not just about individual well-being; it's about maintaining healthy relationships with family, friends, and fellow believers. These relationships are the bedrock of effective ministry and support networks within communities.

Friend, the story of Elijah being almost rejuvenated didn't last forever. He could always return to the source of true rejuvenation. Don't allow yourself to be trapped in a state of being "almost rejuvenated." Embrace the invitation to come before God daily, laying down your burdens and seeking His presence. The closer we draw to Him, the more strength and peace we receive to refresh our spirits.

> "For we which have believed do enter into rest, as he said, As I have sworn in my wrath, if they shall enter into my rest: although the works were finished from the foundation of the world."
>
> Hebrews 4:3

> "There remaineth therefore a rest to the people of God. For he that is entered into his rest, he also hath ceased from his own works, as God did from his."
>
> Hebrews 4:9-10

It's essential to steer clear of that sense of being "almost rejuvenated," which can lead to leaving important tasks unfinished. We mustn't allow anything to obstruct the rest that awaits us in this life or in eternity. We know it's coming, and while the adversary might not always be able to tempt us into sin, he'll strive to push us to overexert ourselves. Thus, it becomes paramount to strike a balance, guarding against procrastination and excessive work so that we can receive the rest we anticipate, which is promised to the people of God.

Not all missed opportunities end in tragedy, but they can teach us lessons. Don't let burnout and exhaustion define your journey. Instead, choose to return to the One who can restore your soul. When the moments come, you need to rest, seek God's presence, and allow Him to rejuvenate you fully. In doing so, you will find the strength to face life's challenges with God's peace that goes beyond understanding.

12

Balaam - Almost Submissive

Balaam as a prophet that we learned about in the Book of Numbers. He would speak things, and it happened. However, he became entangled with greed. Balaam's story showcases his missed opportunity to obey God wholeheartedly, being "almost" submissive to the Most High.

There was a day when Balak, the king of Moab, sought Balaam's assistance in cursing the Israelites; Balaam initially sought the Lord's guidance. A warning came for Balaam not to go with Balak's messengers, as God had already blessed the Israelites. But Balaam's heart was swayed by the promise of wealth and honor. Greed clouded his judgment, and he convinced himself he could negotiate with God to do evil to a people who hadn't done anything to either of them.

Much like the Pharoah in Egypt, Balak feared the people because they were great in number, thinking, "They must be up to something." Someone needs to know not every gathering is about you. The Israelites were on their journey, unaware that the enemy was seeking their demise.

As Balaam journeyed with Balak's officials, God confronted him, intending to deter him from his wicked intentions. However, Balaam remained stubborn and refused to listen to the voice of truth. He allowed his desires to override his better judgment, persisting in his quest for personal gain.

Despite his lack of obedience, God did not abandon trying to reach him. Instead, He sought to communicate through unconventional means. Balaam's journey was interrupted by a talking donkey, who, by God's power, questioned his actions. This divine intervention aimed to shake Balaam out of his self-serving mindset and lead him towards repentance.

Yet, even after this extraordinary encounter, Balaam pursued personal gain. He arrived at Balak's request, who believed he would curse the Israelites, but instead, words of blessing flowed from his mouth. God's truth triumphed, showcasing the power of the Almighty.

Although it seems like Balaam was obedient, he, like many today, was looking for a little wiggle room. Although he didn't curse the people of God, he told Balak how to get them to curse themselves. Why did Balaam do this? For the love of money. God not only looks at what we do, he tries the intentions of our hearts. Somebody desperately needs to know that there is no wiggle room with God. Balaam became almost submissive by telling Balak how to get the people to curse themselves.

> "And the LORD said, My spirit shall not always strive with man, for that he also is flesh: yet his days shall be an hundred and twenty years."
>
> **Genesis 6:3**

It's easy to see people who haven't made God their choice and think, "Did they have a chance?" Just as God was trying to reach this prophet for hire, he knocks at the doors of the hearts of all his people. I often wondered why God continued to talk to Balaam if he used his gift for financial gain. Then, I was reminded that gifts come without repentance. You don't have to be living right to be gifted, but there is a difference between the gift and the anointing.

This story reveals how greed can blind and lead us astray from God's will. Balaam's almost submissive attitude demonstrates the importance of complete alignment with the will of God. Although he didn't do it himself, he gave the enemy the knowledge needed to set up stumbling blocks for the people of God. Balaam conspired against God's people with his actions, making himself an enemy of God.

> "No man can serve two masters: for either he will hate the one, and love the other; or else he will hold to the one, and despise the other. Ye cannot serve God and mammon."
>
> **Matthew 6:24**

When we allow our desires to dictate our actions, we jeopardize the chance to walk in obedience and enjoy the blessings that come from aligning with God's truth. We can learn valuable lessons from Balaam's choices. When we fail to submit to God, we inadvertently yield to the adversary of our souls. Therefore, my friend, I urge you to contemplate your actions carefully. One day, we will all stand before God; every knee shall bow, and every tongue shall confess that Jesus Christ is Lord. The time for wholehearted submission to God is now. Every decision carries consequences, and we cannot afford to live an almost submissive life.

13

David - Almost Ethical

David, the shepherd-turned-king, is one of the most celebrated figures in biblical history. We hear stories of how God took this humble shepherd boy and made him into the king of Israel. With the favor of God upon him, David accomplished great things, including the legendary victory over Goliath and his poetic psalms that continue to touch the hearts of many. Although he had to fight, his kingdom was prosperous and united at the end of his life.

However, even this illustrious king, David, experienced a moment of moral weakness when his judgment faltered. This lapse in judgment led him to miss the opportunity to maintain an ethical position. The story of his affair with Bathsheba and the subsequent plot to have her husband, Uriah, killed left the king in a morally compromised position where his actions were far from ethical.

David allowed desire to cloud his vision and made decisions that violated the principles he once held on to. Instead of turning away from temptation, he succumbed to its allure, setting off a chain of events that would forever tarnish his legacy. His lapse in judgment resulted in the loss of Uriah's life, Bathsheba's suffering, the unraveling of his own family, and the death of many in his kingdom.

> "And the Lord sent Nathan unto David. And he came unto him, and said unto him, There were two men in one city; the one rich, and the other poor. The rich man had exceeding many flocks and herds: But the poor man had nothing, save one little ewe lamb, which he had bought and nourished up: and it grew up together with him, and with his children; it did eat of his own meat, and drank of his own cup, and lay in his bosom, and was unto him as a daughter. And there came a traveller unto the rich man, and he spared to take of his own flock and of his own herd, to dress for the wayfaring man that was come unto him; but took the poor man's lamb, and dressed it for the man that was come to him. And David's anger was greatly kindled against the man; and he said to Nathan, As the Lord liveth, the man that hath done this thing shall surely die: And he shall restore the lamb fourfold, because he did this thing, and because he had no pity. And Nathan said to David, Thou art the man. Thus saith the Lord God of Israel, I anointed thee king over Israel, and I delivered thee out of the hand of Saul; And I gave thee thy master's house, and thy master's wives into thy bosom, and gave thee the house of Israel and of Judah; and if that had been too little, I would moreover have given unto thee such and such things. Wherefore hast thou despised the commandment of the Lord, to do evil in his sight? thou hast killed Uriah the Hittite with the sword, and hast taken his wife to be thy wife, and hast slain him with the sword of the children of Ammon. Now therefore the sword shall never

> depart from thine house; because thou hast despised me, and hast taken the wife of Uriah the Hittite to be thy wife. Thus saith the Lord, Behold, I will raise up evil against thee out of thine own house, and I will take thy wives before thine eyes, and give them unto thy neighbour, and he shall lie with thy wives in the sight of this sun. For thou didst it secretly: but I will do this thing before all Israel, and before the sun. And David said unto Nathan, I have sinned against the Lord. And Nathan said unto David, The Lord also hath put away thy sin; thou shalt not die. Howbeit, because by this deed thou hast given great occasion to the enemies of the Lord to blaspheme, the child also that is born unto thee shall surely die."
>
> 2 Samuel 12:1-14

Lust is a traveler who occasionally comes knocking at the door of our hearts. In the scripture above, we find an illustration of this concept through the story of King David and the prophet Nathan.

In this passage, Nathan tells King David a parable about a rich man who takes the one beloved lamb of a poor man for himself despite having an abundance of sheep. David becomes indignant at this injustice, only for Nathan to reveal to David that he is the rich man in the parable, having taken Uriah's wife, Bathsheba. Often, we tend to be more critical of others than we would be when evaluating ourselves.

Much like that traveler, lust occasionally knocks at the door of our hearts, tempting us to take something that doesn't belong to us. It's a force that can lead us astray, as it did with David. However, this story reminds us that we have a choice. We don't have to let lust in;

we should submit ourselves to God, resist the devil, and guard our hearts with all diligence, as mentioned in Proverbs 4:23. Only when we have protected our minds against the enemy's schemes can we make choices that align with God's will, as the consequences of succumbing to lust can be severe, as David learned from Nathan's rebuke. So, when lust comes knocking, we can keep the door firmly closed, safeguarding our integrity just as we're called to do in our walk of faith.

> "Keep thy heart with all diligence, for out of it are the issues of life."
>
> **Proverbs 4:23**

This missed opportunity to uphold ethical standards reminds us that even the greatest among us are susceptible to moments of weakness and its consequences. It teaches us that our decisions, however small we think them to be, carry weight and can shape our lives.

> "I waited patiently for the Lord; and he inclined unto me, and heard my cry. He brought me up also out of an horrible pit, out of the miry clay, and set my feet upon a rock, and established my goings."
>
> **Psalm 40: 1-2**

In this Psalm, David talks about how he was delivered from a horrible pit where it was hard for him to get proper footing. Yes, sin is a deep ditch. A pit can be so deep it is hard to climb out of.

Similarly, the deeper the descent to sin, the greater the absence of light, thus the more challenging it is to return to level ground. In David's case, we extract valuable lessons regarding decision-making and its repercussions. We are reminded of the importance of ethical conduct and remaining steadfast in our principles, even when faced with temptation. We learn that a single lapse in judgment can affect our relationships and reputation.

If you find yourself trapped in the grip of sin, it may feel like you are in a deep pit, surrounded by darkness and despair. But the beauty of our faith lies in the fact that there is always hope for redemption and restoration.

Just as David, a man after God's own heart, experienced the depths of sin and its consequences, he also discovered the power of repentance and seeking God's forgiveness. When we acknowledge our sinfulness and need for help, we can turn to God with a repentant heart. He is always ready to extend His hand and lift us out of the pit of sin. Just as a friend rushes to the aid of someone in distress, God comes to our rescue when we call out to Him.

> "The righteous cry, and the Lord heareth, and delivereth them out of all their troubles. The Lord is nigh unto them that are of a broken heart; and saveth such as be of a contrite spirit."
>
> Psalm 34:17-18

God is not distant or indifferent to our struggles. He is near those brokenhearted and crushed in spirit, ready to offer comfort, forgiveness, and restoration.

Remember, coming out of sin requires genuine repentance and a desire to turn away from our sinful ways. As we surrender ourselves to Him, He will cleanse us, renew our hearts, and set us on a path of righteousness.

While the consequences of our sins may still linger, God's forgiveness and grace offer us a fresh start. He can take our brokenness and turn it into something beautiful. As we walk in obedience to Him, He will guide, strengthen, and restore us to a place of joy and peace.

So, my friend, there is hope if you find yourself trapped in the pit of sin. You can be lifted from the muck and mire and set on solid ground again. Call God, seek His forgiveness, and allow Him to transform your life.

> "But be doers of the word, and not hearers only, deceiving yourselves. For if anyone is a hearer of the word and not a doer, he is like a man observing his natural face in a mirror; for he observes himself, goes away, and immediately forgets what kind of man he was."
>
> **James 1:22-24**

As followers of Christ, we are called to be self-aware and understand our vulnerabilities and weaknesses. Through this awareness, we can identify areas that need strengthening and growth. By recognizing our shortcomings, we can intentionally address them and align ourselves more closely with God's will.

Being doers of the Word means hearing and understanding God's teachings and actively living them out in our daily lives. It is a call to walk in holiness, strive for righteousness, and embody the values and principles God has revealed to us through His Word.

In our pursuit of holiness, we are challenged to go beyond mere external actions and appearances. It is not enough to go through the motions of ethical behavior or be "almost ethical" in our actions. God desires our hearts to be transformed, our motives to be pure, and our actions to be aligned with His perfect standards.

To avoid being "almost ethical," we must examine our hearts and motives. We must seek to understand the underlying reasons behind our actions and ensure that they are rooted in love, integrity, and a genuine desire to honor God. Being ethical requires constantly evaluating our thoughts, attitudes, and intentions, allowing the Holy Spirit to convict and guide us.

Walking in holiness also involves a commitment to ongoing growth and transformation. It is a lifelong journey of surrendering ourselves to God's work in us, allowing Him to shape and mold us into His image. This requires humility, openness, and a willingness to confront our weaknesses and areas of vulnerability.

As we strive to be doers of the Word and walk in holiness, we can draw strength from God's grace and the power of His Spirit within us. Through the leading of His Spirit, we can overcome our weaknesses, resist temptation, and live lives pleasing to Him. By strengthening ourselves where needed and walking in holiness, we can avoid the trap of being "almost ethical" in our actions. Let us continually seek God's guidance, rely on His grace, and allow His transformative work to shape us into the image-bearers He has called us to be.

14

Solomon - Almost Steadfast

While Solomon, the wisest man on earth, was blessed with wisdom and favor from God, his story took a tragic turn in his old age, highlighting his missed opportunity to remain faithful to God and the consequences of prioritizing wealth, power, and women over spiritual values.

> "In Gibeon the Lord appeared to Solomon in a dream by night. God said, Ask what I shall give thee.
>
> Solomon replied, You have shown great mercy to my father David, as he walked in truth, righteousness, and uprightness of heart before you. You've kept the kindness by giving him a son to sit on his throne, as it is today.
>
> Now, O Lord my God, you've made me king instead of my father David, and I am but a little child. I don't know how to

go out or come in. Your servant is among your chosen people, a vast multitude that cannot be counted.

Solomon requested, Give me an understanding heart to judge your people, so I can discern between good and bad. Who can judge such a great people?

The Lord was pleased with Solomon's request, and God said, Because you asked for understanding to discern judgment and not for long life, riches, or the life of your enemies, I have given you a wise and understanding heart. No one before you or after you will be like you.

I have also granted you riches and honor beyond what you asked for, so that no king will surpass you during your lifetime.

God added, If you walk in my ways, keep my statutes and commandments, as your father David did walk, I will lengthen your days."

1 Kings 3:5-14

Solomon's Extraordinary Wisdom and Knowledge

The following verses offer a glimpse into the remarkable wisdom and knowledge bestowed upon King Solomon by God. Through these passages, we witness Solomon's extraordinary intellectual capabilities surpassing his peers during his time.

"And God gave Solomon wisdom and understanding exceeding much, and largeness of heart, even as the sand that is on the sea shore. And Solomon's wisdom excelled the wisdom of all the children of the east country, and all the wisdom of Egypt. For he was wiser than all men; than Ethan the Ezrahite, and Heman, and Chalcol, and Darda, the sons of Mahol: and his fame was in all nations round about. And he spake three thousand proverbs: and his songs were a thousand and five. And he spake of trees, from the cedar tree that is in Lebanon even unto the hyssop that springeth out of the wall: he spake also of beasts, and of fowl, and of creeping things, and of fishes. And there came of all people to hear the wisdom of Solomon, from all kings of the earth, which had heard of his wisdom."

1 Kings 4:29-34

"For the Lord gives wisdom; from his mouth come knowledge and understanding. He holds success in store for the upright, he is a shield to those whose walk is blameless."

Proverbs 2:6-7

Solomon began his reign as a young man with a humble spirit and devotion to God. He understood the importance of seeking wisdom and discernment, and righteous choices marked his early years. He authored much of the Book of Proverbs, imparting knowledge to future generations.

Solomon's Love for Foreign Women

Solomon's heart began to wander as time passed, and he moved away from the wisdom that once defined his reign. In the opening verses of 1 Kings 11, we see King Solomon's love for foreign women, including the daughter of Pharaoh and women from various nations. These unions were against the Lord's commands.

> "And the LORD stirred up an adversary unto Solomon, Hadad the Edomite: he was of the king's seed in Edom. For it came to pass, when David was in Edom, and Joab the captain of the host was gone up to bury the slain, after he had smitten every male in Edom; (For six months did Joab remain there with all Israel, until he had cut off every male in Edom:) That Hadad fled, he and certain Edomites of his father's servants with him, to go into Egypt; Hadad being yet a little child. And they arose out of Midian, and came to Paran: and they took men with them out of Paran, and they came to Egypt, unto Pharaoh king of Egypt; which gave him an house, and appointed him victuals, and gave him land. And Hadad found great favour in the sight of Pharaoh, so that he gave him to wife the sister of his own wife, the sister of Tahpenes the queen. And the sister of Tahpenes bare him Genubath his son, whom Tahpenes weaned in Pharaoh's house: and Genubath was in Pharaoh's household among the sons of Pharaoh.
>
> And when Hadad heard in Egypt that David slept with his fathers, and that Joab the captain of the host was dead, Hadad said to Pharaoh, Let me depart, that I may go to mine own country. Then Pharaoh said unto him, But what hast thou lacked with me, that, behold, thou seekest to go to thine

own country? And he answered, Nothing: howbeit let me go in any wise."

1 Kings 11:1-8

The Lord's Anger and Consequences

This section shows the Lord's anger towards Solomon due to his departure from God's ways. The consequences of Solomon's actions are revealed, including the prophecy of Ahijah.

"And the LORD was angry with Solomon because his heart had turned away from the LORD, the God of Israel, who had appeared to him twice and had commanded him concerning this thing, that he should not go after other gods. But he did not keep what the LORD commanded. Therefore the LORD said to Solomon, 'Since this has been your practice and you have not kept my covenant and my statutes that I have commanded you, I will surely tear the kingdom from you and will give it to your servant. Yet for the sake of David your father, I will not do it in your days, but I will tear it out of the hand of your son. However, I will not tear away all the kingdom, but I will give one tribe to your son, for the sake of David my servant and for the sake of Jerusalem that I have chosen.'

And the LORD raised up an adversary against Solomon, Hadad the Edomite. He was of the royal house in Edom. For when David was in Edom, and Joab the commander of the army went up to bury the slain, he struck down every male in Edom (for Joab and all Israel remained there six months, until he had cut off every male in Edom). But Hadad fled to Egypt, together with certain Edomites of his father's servants, Hadad still being a little child. They set out from Midian and came to Paran and took men with them from Paran and came to Egypt, to Pharaoh king of Egypt, who gave him a house and assigned him an allowance of food and gave him land.

And Hadad found great favor in the sight of Pharaoh, so that he gave him in marriage the sister of his own wife, the sister of Tahpenes the queen. And the sister of Tahpenes bore him Genubath his son, whom Tahpenes weaned in Pharaoh's house. And Genubath was in Pharaoh's house among the sons of Pharaoh. But when Hadad heard in Egypt that David slept with his fathers and that Joab the commander of the army was dead, Hadad said to Pharaoh, 'Let me depart, that I may go to my own country.'"

1 Kings 11:9-20

The Rise of Adversaries

This part introduces an adversary named Hadad, an Edomite, who becomes a challenge to Solomon's reign. The political landscape begins to shift.

"But when Hadad heard in Egypt that David slept with his fathers and that Joab the commander of the army was dead, Hadad said to Pharaoh, 'Let me depart, that I may go to my own country.' But Pharaoh said to him, 'What have you lacked with me that you are now seeking to go to your own country?' And he said, 'Only let me depart.'

Now God raised up another adversary against Solomon, Rezon the son of Eliada, who had fled from his master Hadadezer king of Zobah. He gathered men about him and became leader of a marauding band after the killing by David. And they went to Damascus and lived there and made him king in Damascus. He was an adversary of Israel all the days of Solomon, doing harm as Hadad did. And he loathed Israel and reigned over Syria."

1 Kings 11:21-25

Division of the Kingdom

Jeroboam, a significant figure, rises against Solomon. We see the prophecy of Ahijah regarding the division of the kingdom and the continued turmoil during Solomon's reign.

"Also, Jeroboam the son of Nebat, an Ephraimite of Zereda, a servant of Solomon, whose mother's name was Zeruah, a widow, rebelled against the king. And this was the reason why he rebelled against the king. Solomon built the Millo, and closed up the breach of the city of David his father. The man Jeroboam was very able, and when Solomon saw that the young man was industrious, he gave him charge over all the forced labor of the house of Joseph.

And at that time, when Jeroboam went out of Jerusalem, the prophet Ahijah the Shilonite found him on the road. Now Ahijah had dressed himself in a new garment, and the two of them were alone in the open country. Then Ahijah laid hold of the new garment that was on him, and tore it into twelve pieces. And he said to Jeroboam, 'Take for yourself ten pieces, for thus says the LORD, the God of Israel, "Behold, I am about to tear the kingdom from the hand of Solomon and will give you ten tribes (but he shall have one tribe, for the sake of my servant David and for the sake of Jerusalem, the city that I have chosen out of all the tribes of Israel), because they have forsaken me and worshiped Ashtoreth the goddess of the Sidonians, Chemosh the god of Moab, and Milcom the god of the Ammonites, and they have not walked in my ways, doing what is right in my sight and keeping my statutes and my rules, as David his father did.'

Nevertheless, I will not take the whole kingdom out of his hand, but I will make him ruler all the days of his life, for the sake of David my servant whom I chose, who kept my commandments and my statutes. But I will take the kingdom out of his son's hand and will give it to you, ten tribes. Yet to his son I will give one tribe, that David my servant may always have a lamp before me in Jerusalem, the city where I have chosen to put my name. And I will take you, and you shall reign over all that your soul desires, and you shall be king over Israel. And if you will listen to all that I command you, and will walk in my ways, and do what is right in my eyes by keeping my statutes and my commandments, as David my servant did, I will be with you and will build you a

> sure house, as I built for David, and I will give Israel to you. And I will afflict the offspring of David because of this, but not forever.'
>
> Solomon sought therefore to kill Jeroboam. But Jeroboam arose and fled into Egypt, to Shishak king of Egypt, and was in Egypt until the death of Solomon."
>
> 1 Kings 11:26-40

Solomon's missed opportunity lay in his failure to remain obedient and steadfast in his faith. He allowed his desires and ambitions to dictate his choices rather than seeking God's will. In doing so, he compromised his spiritual values and lost sight of the source of wisdom and fulfillment.

In the Book of Ecclesiastes, believed to have been written by Solomon in his old age, he reflects on the vanity of earthly pursuits. He realizes that his accumulation of wealth, power, and worldly pleasures has left him empty and disillusioned. Solomon concludes that true wisdom is to fear God and keep His commandments, a realization that came late in his life.

This story reminds us of prioritizing spiritual values over worldly pursuits. It teaches us that wisdom is not a momentary concept but a steadfast virtue that requires continuous pursuit.

Let's take a closer look at wisdom:

In the book of Proverbs, Solomon emphasizes that wisdom is always present and accessible to those who seek it. He reminds us that wisdom is not limited by time, place, or circumstance. It is readily available to all who earnestly desire it.

> "The way of life is above to the wise, that he may depart from hell beneath."
>
> **Proverbs 15:24**

> "Wisdom is too high for a fool: he openeth not his mouth in the gate."
>
> **Proverbs 24:7**

In Proverbs, Solomon emphasizes that wisdom is always present. It's in the same place for the righteous as for the fool. That means it doesn't move away from you. Instead, you move away from it. The only reason it is too high for a fool is their unwillingness to reach for it. At any moment, a fool can become wise if they start reaching. Likewise, a wise man can become a fool when they are no longer reaching for God.

> "Wisdom is the principal thing; therefore get wisdom: and with all thy getting get understanding. Exalt her, and she shall promote thee: she shall bring thee to honour, when thou dost embrace her. She shall give to thine head an ornament of grace: a crown of glory shall she deliver to thee."
>
> **Proverbs 4:7-9**

In the end, Solomon's life teaches us a valuable lesson. His journey from wisdom and greatness to foolishness and neglect of his spiritual well-being reminds us of the danger of putting worldly desires ahead of our spiritual health. While Solomon was once very committed to gaining wisdom, his later choices led him away from the right path. We should take this as a lesson and remember that true fulfillment and wisdom come from fearing God and keeping His commandments. I pray that we never become 'almost steadfast' in our quest for wisdom but stay determined in our dedication to God.

Solomon's failure to actively pursue wisdom left him vulnerable to his foolishness. Folly can take many forms, including making unwise decisions, ignoring the consequences of our actions, or neglecting to consider the long-term effects. Solomon ultimately fell short despite initially showing great promise in his pursuit of wisdom.

The story of Solomon serves as both a cautionary tale and a call to action. We are called to diligently seek wisdom, placing it as a top priority in our lives. Doing so requires seeking guidance from God and making His will our ultimate focus. By doing so, we can avoid the dangers of folly and prevent ourselves from merely coming close to steadfastness in our pursuit of wisdom. Instead, we can wholeheartedly and unwaveringly pursue wisdom, allowing it to shape our thoughts, actions, and decisions.

15

Laban - Almost Fulfilled

At a time when many were deeply immersed in idol worship, our story revolves around a man whose life was centered around these beliefs. Like numerous others, he practiced idol worship and passed down these traditions to his family. Naturally, children are influenced by the beliefs instilled in them during their upbringing. However, when his nephew came to live with him, he began to see the God of Abraham and Isaac at work.

This man had a encounter with the Most High during the quiet hours of the night. Laban found himself engaged in a dialogue with God regarding his son-in-law, Jacob. This experience revealed a power far more profound than anything he had ever encountered through his man-made idols. The idols he worshiped were incapable of such direct communication with him.

> "They have ears, but they hear not: noses have they, but they smell not."
>
> **Psalms 115:6**

Think about it, Laban had a conversation with the maker of the ends of the earth. This conversation should have sparked a profound curiosity and a deeper longing for understanding in his heart. Many who don't follow God feel as if they are doing the right thing. Feeling right and being right are totally different.

> "There is a way that seems right to a man, but its end is the way to death."
>
> **Proverbs 14:12**

However, even with this encounter, Laban faced challenges in wholeheartedly accepting the reality before him. His perspective remained obscured by the injustice he believed Jacob had committed against him. His ability to see beyond his sense of betrayal was hindered, and he aimed to recover what he thought was maliciously taken. When speaking to Jacob, he told of how the God of his fathers had appeared to him, but a question followed:

> "And now, though thou wouldest needs be gone, because thou sore longedst after thy father's house, yet wherefore hast thou stolen my gods?"
>
> **Genesis 31:30**

It was hard for Laban to receive the encounter because of what was done to him. Little did he know that genuine connection was still within his grasp. His story serves as a caution for all who would pursue God. You don't have to leave the presence of God almost fulfilled. There is a song that says, "Don't let nothing shake your faith in God." How often has it been hard to follow God because of the people who profess Him? I often tell my son even if everyone is doing wrong, you do right. People are watching you. Laban was watching Jacob. He was close to experiencing a genuine relationship with the Most High, yet his unresolved bitterness towards Jacob kept him trapped, "almost fulfilled."

> "Brethren, I count not myself to have apprehended: but this one thing I do, forgetting those things which are behind, and reaching forth unto those things which are before, I press toward the mark for the prize of the high calling of God in Christ Jesus."
>
> **Philippians 3:13-14**

Are we pursuing our former gods, those idols that promise fulfillment but ultimately leave us empty? Are there areas where we cling to past hurts? It may be stopping us from going to the next level in God, or worse. Maybe we've prevented others from seeing the goodness of the Lord in the land of the living. God is not willing that any should perish, but all come to repentance. Friend, don't let what people have done in the past prevent you from embracing God, who has the power to transform.

> "Therefore, if thou bring thy gift to the altar, and there rememberest that thy brother hath ought against thee, leave there thy gift before the altar, and go thy way; first be reconciled to thy brother, and then come and offer thy gift."
>
> Matthew 5:23-24

To speak with God is a life-changing event. In this story, it should have been a motivation for change. It should have led him to let go of his grievances and seek reconciliation. Yet, he allowed his anger and bitterness to hinder his progress. As we travel our paths, draw wisdom from the story of Laban. Take a good look within, and let go of any lingering resentment or grievances obstructing your walk with God. Stay vigilant against the temptations of our past idols, and choose to follow the one true God who provides fulfillment.

> "Let your light so shine before men, that they may see your good works, and glorify your Father which is in heaven."
>
> Matthew 15:16

Strive to walk in a way where others may see our good works and glorify the mighty God of Heaven. Live in a way that draws others to God. In addition, don't allow our perspective of others to cloud our vision of who God is. By doing so, we can move beyond the confines of living an "almost fulfilled" life.

16

The Israelites - Almost Believed

The story of God's chosen people, the Israelites, is one of many highs and lows. For centuries, they endured the hardships that accompanied captivity in Egypt, longing for freedom and the fulfillment of promises until the day that God sent a deliverer. In a magnificent display, the Most High demonstrated his power and authority over every god worshipped in Egypt, sending plagues upon them. He parted the Red Sea and led His people out of the land of their captivity with a mighty outstretched hand. Who else could cause them to walk across the sea on dry ground?

However, despite witnessing the miracles and experiencing the faithfulness of the Lord, they struggled with unbelief. The people questioned Moses and their Creator. Instead of recounting the miraculous deeds they witnessed as God brought them out, they remembered their comforts in captivity.

> "We remember the fish, which we did eat in Egypt freely; the cucumbers, and the melons, and the leeks, and the onions, and the garlic."
>
> Numbers 11:5

> "And there we saw the giants, the sons of Anak, which come of the giants: and we were in our own sight as grasshoppers, and so we were in their sight."
>
> Numbers 13:33

> "Say unto them, As truly as I live, saith the Lord, as ye have spoken in mine ears, so will I do to you: Your carcases shall fall in this wilderness; and all that were numbered of you, according to your whole number, from twenty years old and upward which have murmured against me, Doubtless ye shall not come into the land, concerning which I sware to make you dwell therein, save Caleb the son of Jephunneh, and Joshua the son of Nun. But your little ones, which ye said should be a prey, them will I bring in, and they shall know the land which ye have despised."
>
> Numbers 14:28-31

Fear gripped their hearts when they arrived at the threshold of the Promised Land. Magnifying the enemy over the King of Kings, they doubted God's ability to conquer the land's inhabitants, failing to trust His promises and provision. These were the same people who witnessed the cloud by day and the fire by night. This lack of faith led to a tragic consequence - except for two men, all those who were twenty and up, an entire generation of unbelievers were condemned to wander in the wilderness until their demise.

> "But my servant Caleb, because he had another spirit with him, and hath followed me fully, him will I bring into the land whereinto he went; and his seed shall possess it."
>
> **Numbers 14:24**

This case study reminds us that unbelief can hinder the fulfillment of God's promises in our lives. They were on the brink of entering into the abundant blessings that were prepared for them, yet their lack of faith prevented them from experiencing the fullness of His provision. All they had to do was remember what God did for them. They didn't even have to think too far back. These miracles had just happened.

The quote says:

> "Watch your thoughts, they become your words. watch your words, they become your actions. watch your actions, they become your habits. watch your habits, they become your character. watch your character, it becomes your destiny."- Lao Tzu

If words are spirits, accepting them will have a manifestation in your life. Although the 12 spies went in, the Bible says that two trusted God, and Caleb had another spirit. How did he get another spirit? He chose it. Remember, fear is a spirit. Listen, if fear is trying to invade you, you must choose another spirit. Some lots in life we accept. With the enemy, you never have to take the things you are given.

"For God hath not given us the spirit of fear, but of power, and of love, and of a sound mind."

2 Timothy 1:7

"Finally, brethren, whatsoever things are true, whatsoever things are honest, whatsoever things are just, whatsoever things are pure, whatsoever things are lovely, whatsoever things are of good report; if there be any virtue, and if there be any praise, think on these things."

Philippians 4:8

"Wherefore (as the Holy Ghost saith, To day if ye will hear his voice, Harden not your hearts, as in the provocation, in the day of temptation in the wilderness: When your fathers tempted me, proved me, and saw my works forty years. Wherefore I was grieved with that generation, and said, They do alway err in their heart; and they have not known my ways. So I sware in my wrath, They shall not enter into my rest.)"

Hebrews 3:7-11

> "So we see that they could not enter in because of unbelief."
>
> **Hebrews 3:19**

In our lives, we encounter similar moments of decision and faith. God invites us to walk in His promises to embrace the blessings He has in store for us. Yet, like the Israelites, many are tempted to doubt, to allow unbelief to hold us back from entering into the abundant life He has promised. The lesson from the Israelites is clear: we must not let unbelief hinder us. Confront any doubts or fears, and choose to trust in the power and faithfulness of God. Instead of dwelling in the wilderness of unbelief, we must step forward in faith, claiming God's promises.

> "But let him ask in faith, nothing wavering. For he that wavereth is like a wave of the sea driven with the wind and tossed. For let not that man think that he shall receive anything of the Lord."
>
> **James 1:6-7**

> "Jesus answered and said unto them, Verily I say unto you, If ye have faith, and doubt not, ye shall not only do this which is done to the fig tree, but also if ye shall say unto this mountain, Be thou removed, and be thou cast into the sea; it shall be done. And all things, whatsoever ye shall ask in prayer, believing, ye shall receive."
>
> **Matthew 21:21-22**

> "He staggered not at the promise of God through unbelief; but was strong in faith, giving glory to God; And being fully persuaded that, what he had promised, he was able also to perform."
>
> Romans 4:20-21

> "Jesus said unto him, If thou canst believe, all things are possible to him that believeth. And straightway the father of the child cried out, and said with tears, Lord, I believe; help thou mine unbelief."
>
> Mark 9:23-24

Are there areas of unbelief that we need to confront in examining ourselves? Are there promises that God has spoken over our lives that we have hesitated to embrace? Like the man with the demon-possessed son, we may have to pray, "help my unbelief." We can see mountains move and enter the promise if we trust God. When talking about belief, I feel obligated to say that faith is not passive but active - it requires us to step forward, to believe in the unseen, and to hold on to it until we see it.

So many start on journeys where it's promising; they see God move and fight battles, and somewhere along the way, they forget. The word "remember" is in the Bible 231 times. God set up celebrations periodically throughout the year to remind the people it was time to return to Him.

Significant feasts in for the Israelites:

Passover

This celebration commemorates the Israelites' liberation from slavery in Egypt. It includes a special meal called the Seder, during which the story of the Exodus is retold.

Feast of Unleavened Bread

This feast immediately follows Passover and lasts seven days. It represents the haste with which the Israelites left Egypt.

Note: Yeast, which represents sin, was to be removed from each dwelling, symbolizing our journey of perfecting. If we are to depart to our promised land, we must deal with the issue of sin in our temples.

> "Your glorying is not good. Know ye not that a little leaven leaveneth the whole lump?"
>
> 1 Corinthians 5:6

Feast of Firstfruits

During the Passover season, this feast offered the barley harvest's first fruits to God. It was a way of expressing gratitude for the harvest and recognizing God's provision.

Pentecost

Also known as the Feast of Weeks, Pentecost takes place fifty days after Passover, typically in May or June. It was originally instituted to acknowledge the giving of the Law (the Ten Commandments) to Moses on Mount Sinai and later the firstfruits of the wheat harvest.

Note: When they were in the wilderness, Israel did not need to plant. God provided for them. After they left, they planted and added the commemoration of the firstfruits in their celebration. Before that, this celebration was to thank God for his Word.

Feast of Trumpets

This festival marks the start of the Jewish civil year, usually in September or October. During this feast, they blow the trumpets (shofars), and it is seen as a time of reflection, repentance, and preparation for the upcoming Day of Atonement.

We hear of celebrations and parties for the new year, but in Jewish culture these holidays were Holy Days. It wasn't to meet up with people you hadn't seen in a long time, but times for reconciliation with God. So God established a feast lest we forget that this time is dedicated to getting right with Him.

Day of Atonement

Yom Kippur falls ten days after the Feast of Trumpets, in September or October. It is a solemn day of fasting, prayer, and repentance, where sins are confessed and atonement is sought from God.

Feast of Tabernacles

Celebrated in the fall, typically in September or October, Sukkot lasts seven days and commemorates the Israelites' time in the wilderness. During this feast, people dwell in temporary shelters called sukkahs.

Remembering their wilderness journey and dwelling in sukkahs reminded the Israelites of the dangers of fear and unbelief. Remember: Fear and lack of trust in God's promises led to many not entering the Promised Land. Sukkot provided an annual opportunity for reflection on this lesson and encouraged trust in God's guidance and protection.

Feast of Dedication

Hanukkah, also known as the Festival of Lights, occurs in December. It commemorates the rededication of the Second Temple in Jerusalem after it was desecrated. It serves as a reminder of the miracle of the oil lasting eight days in the menorah when there was only enough oil for one day.

It teaches us that God can provide a way forward even in challenging circumstances or when we have limited resources. Hanukkah reminds us that we can always begin again, and God is there to help and guide us.

Celebrations often trigger happy emotions, which are directly tied to our memory. Considering each feast the Israelites celebrated pointed them back to God, brings up another question. Where do your celebrations lead? I pray you take the time to consider this question.

> "Ask and it shall be given you; seek, and ye shall find; knock, and it shall be opened unto you: For every one that asketh receiveth; and he that seeketh findeth; and to him that knocketh it shall be opened."
>
> **Matthew 7:7-8**

What should we do when our faith is tested before we get to the promise? We keep Going! We keep knocking! We keep asking, and we keep seeking! For everyone who continues to knock, the doors will continue to be opened to them. Everyone who continues to ask will continue to get answers! Everyone who continues to seek will continue to find. The blessing is in the act of persisting, even when the odds seem to be stacked against you. Persist.

> "Now faith is the substance of things hoped for, the evidence of things not seen."
>
> **Hebrews 11:1**

> "But without faith it is impossible to please him: for he that cometh to God must believe that he is, and that he is a rewarder of them that diligently seek him."
>
> **Hebrews 11:6**

"By faith Noah, being warned of God of things not seen as yet, moved with fear, prepared an ark to the saving of his house; by the which he condemned the world and became heir of the righteousness which is by faith."

Hebrews 11:7

"By faith Abraham, when he was called to go out into a place which he should after receive for an inheritance, obeyed; and he went out, not knowing whither he went."

Hebrews 11:8

"By faith they passed through the Red sea as by dry land: which the Egyptians assaying to do were drowned."

Hebrews 11:29

"By faith the walls of Jericho fell down, after they were compassed about seven days."

Hebrews 11:30

> "And these all, having obtained a good report through faith, received not the promise: God having provided some better thing for us, that they without us should not be made perfect."
>
> Hebrews 11:39-40

We should learn from the Israelites who almost believed and let us choose to have an unwavering faith in God's promises. Press on, refusing to let unbelief hinder your journey toward living an abundant life in Christ Jesus. So many promises are waiting for the one who believes that God is a rewarder of them who diligently seek Him.

17

Thief on the Cross - Almost Redeemed

When we think of the cross, many only think of Jesus and the price he paid. We often recall the one thief, burdened with guilt and an awareness of his impending fate, who seized the last-minute opportunity for redemption.

Imagine being on the cross with Jesus as he's being openly mocked by a crowd yelling insults. This thief did not have a chance to steal away in secret and ask for prayer. The man had to shout over others to be heard. In the face of condemnation, he humbly turned to Jesus and publicly acknowledged His innocence, recognizing that they deserved their punishment while Jesus was without fault. With genuine repentance, the thief implored,

> "Lord, remember me when thou comest into thy kingdom."
>
> **Luke 23:42**

Jesus, moved by the sincerity and faith of the repentant thief, responded with compassion, assuring him,

> "...Verily I say unto thee, Today shalt thou be with me in paradise."
>
> Luke 23:43

In that instant, the thief's life was forever changed, his eternity secured by the forgiving love of Christ. This is a beautiful story of how Jesus paused what he was doing for all mankind to save a man who was undoubtedly on his way to hell.

Yet, that isn't the thief we focus on in this tale of missed opportunities. Alongside this redeemed thief, there was another who remained unrepentant. Despite witnessing the same scene and hearing the words of Jesus, this other thief chose not to seek forgiveness. He clung to his pride and bitterness, missing the chance for redemption that was within his grasp.

From 9:00 a.m. to 3:00 p.m., Jesus was on the cross between the two thieves. It was around 3:00 p.m. that the one thief cried out in repentance. Although they were only on the cross for six hours, both had a small window of opportunity for salvation. It wasn't a grand announcement; there was no countdown, but he missed it when it happened. Although the window of opportunity was small, it was there. All have a chance to turn to God, yet many remain almost redeemed.

The story of the thief on the cross teaches us about the present moment and the urgency of seeking God while he may be found. It reminds us that no matter how dire our circumstances may seem, there is always a chance for redemption. Just don't let it slip through your fingers.

> "To day if ye will hear his voice, Harden not your heart, as in the provocation, and as in the day of temptation in the wilderness:"
>
> Psalm 95:8

The day of provocation was when the children of Israel did not believe God, thus missing out on the promised land. Jesus came to seek and save the lost, offering forgiveness and eternal life to all who turn to Him, yet time and chance happen to them all.

We are called to live pleasing to God, yet if we sin, we have an advocate with the Father. When we find ourselves tempted to live unholy, we must remember that sin has repercussions. These two men on the cross had to deal with the consequences of their sins, yet hope appeared as their lives were drawing to an end.

Don't miss your moment! What moment am I talking about, your moment to be redeemed. You don't have to settle for only seeing others receive God and never getting Him for yourself. The song says, "there is room at the cross for you."

> "For I am persuaded, that neither death, nor life, nor angels, nor principalities, nor powers, nor things present, nor things to come, nor height, nor depth, nor any other creature, shall be able to separate us from the love of God, which is in Christ Jesus our Lord."
>
> Romans 8:38-39

The story of the thief on the cross helps us recognize that each moment is precious, and we must ensure we are ready to see God in peace. What profit is it in gaining the world and losing your soul? We brought nothing into this world and we can't take anything out. The only thing we will have for eternity is our soul. If you neglect it now, you'll wish you made better choices later. What stood between this other thief and eternal life? It was the same for both of them. They faced embarrassment, looks of shame, and pride. What are you going to let separate you from the love of Christ? Friend, I'm trying to say it's too late in the day to let anything cause you to be almost redeemed. Count up the cost. Whatever it is, is it worth eternity?

18

The Rich Man - Almost Compassionate

In one of His parables, Jesus shared the story of a rich man and a beggar named Lazarus. It's important to note that this wasn't a made-up story; These were people who lived, and Jesus spoke of an event that actually happened. The rich man lived a life of luxury and abundance, while Lazarus was destitute, lying at the rich man's gate, covered in sores and longing for even a morsel of food. Despite their contrasting circumstances, the rich man missed a crucial opportunity to show compassion and extend a helping hand to Lazarus.

God commanded His people to care for the poor and the needy, to demonstrate love and empathy towards the less fortunate. However, the rich man was consumed by his wealth and indulgence, blind to the suffering of Lazarus right outside his doorstep. He was almost compassionate, but his indifference prevented him from taking action.

> "There was a certain rich man, which was clothed in purple and fine linen, and fared sumptuously every day: And there was a certain beggar named Lazarus, which was laid at his gate, full of sores, And desiring to be fed with the crumbs which fell from the rich man's table: moreover the dogs came and licked his sores."
>
> Luke 16:19-21

Tragically, both the rich man and Lazarus eventually passed away. In eternity, their situations were reversed. Lazarus found himself in the comforting embrace of Abraham while the rich man was tormented in Hades. In anguish, the rich man pleaded with Abraham to send Lazarus to relieve him of his suffering, but it was too late. The opportunity to show compassion had slipped away, and the consequences of his indifference were dire.

This parable reminds us of the importance of compassion and empathy. It calls us to examine our attitudes and actions towards those in need. Like the rich man, will we turn a blind eye to the suffering around us, or will we choose to be compassionate and extend a helping hand?

Jesus reminds us that our treatment of others reflects our relationship with God Himself. Our choices to embrace or ignore those in need have eternal implications. It is not enough to be almost compassionate; we are called to display the love and kindness that Christ has shown us.

As we consider the parable of the rich man and Lazarus, let us reflect on our lives. Are we aware of the suffering and needs of those around us? Are we actively seeking opportunities to show compassion, to be the hands and feet of Jesus in a broken world? Will we allow empathy to move us to action, or will we remain indifferent and miss out on spiritual growth and the opportunity to impact lives for eternity?

> "Jesus said unto him, Thou shalt love the Lord thy God with all thy heart, and with all thy soul, and with all thy mind. This is the first and great commandment. And the second is like unto it, Thou shalt love thy neighbor as thyself. On these two commandments hang all the law and the prophets."
>
> Matthew 22:37-40

> "What doth it profit, my brethren, though a man say he hath faith, and have not works? can faith save him? If a brother or sister be naked, and destitute of daily food, And one of you say unto them, Depart in peace, be ye warmed and filled; notwithstanding ye give them not those things which are needful to the body; what doth it profit? Even so faith, if it hath not works, is dead, being alone."
>
> James 2:14-17

The choice is ours. It's not enough to be almost compassionate. We must be fully committed to living out the command to love our neighbors as ourselves. For one day, we will stand before God, and He will reveal the true nature of our hearts and our actions towards others.

Imagine standing before the Lord with accusations against you.

> "For I was an hungered, and ye gave me no meat: I was thirsty, and ye gave me no drink: I was a stranger, and ye took me not in: naked, and ye clothed me not: sick, and in prison, and ye visited me not. Then shall they also answer him, saying, Lord, when saw we thee an hungered, or athirst, or a stranger, or naked, or sick, or in prison, and did not minister unto thee? Then shall he answer them, saying, Verily I say unto you, Inasmuch as ye did it not to one of the least of these, ye did it not to me. And these shall go away into everlasting punishment: but the righteous into life eternal."
>
> **Matthews 25:42-46**

This is not an attempt to scare you. It's a plea for those who need to alter their behaviors. Don't settle for being almost compassionate. It simply isn't enough! God is calling us to a higher standard of living and loving.

The parable of the rich man and Lazarus should serve as a wake-up call for all of us. We are challenged to examine our hearts and actions towards those who are less fortunate. True compassion goes beyond sympathy or acknowledgement of someone's suffering. It requires us to actively engage and make a difference in their lives.

In the parable, the rich man had every opportunity to show compassion to Lazarus, but he chose to ignore him. He was so consumed by his own wealth and comfort that he failed to see the desperate need right at his doorstep. This indifference ultimately led to his own downfall. In eternity, while Lazarus found comfort and solace, the rich man faced torment and regret. Our choices in this life have eternal implications. How we treat others, especially those in need, reflects our relationship with God.

Jesus Himself emphasized the importance of compassion and love for our neighbors.

> "Jesus said unto him, Thou shalt love the Lord thy God with all thy heart, and with all thy soul, and with all thy mind. This is the first and great commandment. And the second is like unto it, Thou shalt love thy neighbour as thyself. On these two commandments hang all the law and the prophets."
>
> Matthew 22:37-40

The greatest commandments are to love God with all our heart, soul, and mind, and to love our neighbors as ourselves. These commandments encompass all the teachings of the law and the prophets. It is a call to action, to actively demonstrate our love for God by loving and caring for those around us.

> "What doth it profit, my brethren, though a man say he hath faith, and have not works? can faith save him? If a brother or sister be naked, and destitute of daily food, And one of you say unto them, Depart in peace, be ye warmed and filled; notwithstanding ye give them not those things which are needful to the body; what doth it profit? Even so faith, if it hath not works, is dead, being alone."
>
> James 2:14-17

The apostle James reminds us that faith without works is dead. It is not enough to simply have faith or to offer empty words of comfort to those in need. True faith is demonstrated through our actions and willingness to meet the practical needs of others.

Friend, I pray we won't settle for being almost compassionate. We must strive to be fully committed to living out the command to love our neighbors as ourselves. Let us open our eyes to the suffering and needs of those around us and actively seek opportunities to make a difference. By doing so, we not only impact lives in the present, but we also store up treasures in heaven.

I pray we become a people who are known for our compassion, empathy, and love. That we become the hands and feet of Jesus in a broken world, bringing hope and healing to those who need it most. Let us never forget that our actions towards others are ultimately a reflection of our love for God. Let us remember that being almost compassionate is not enough; it falls short of the standard of love that we are called to. Instead, lets strive to be fully compassionate, actively seeking ways to alleviate the suffering of others and make a positive impact in their lives for the glory of God.

19

The Rich Young Ruler - Almost Unburdened

In the region of Judea, a rich young ruler approached Jesus with a question about eternal life. This question about what happens in the "life after" is rooted in the human desire for meaning, the fear of death, and the search for more. It offers a sense of continuity and hope beyond our earthly existence. This young ruler, brought up under Jewish teachings desired the rest that the prophets talked about. Exploring the concept of the afterlife allows us to confront our mortality, seek answers to existential questions, and find solace in the belief that there is something more to our journey beyond this life.

> "And behold, one came and said unto him, Good Master, what good thing shall I do, that I may have eternal life?"
>
> Matthew 19:16

This young man had achieved great wealth and earthly success, yet deep down, he sensed something was missing. Jesus, seeing the sincerity in the young man's heart, responded with love and wisdom. Often, when we read this, we can overlook what Jesus said,

> "And he said unto him, Why callest thou me good? there is none good but one, that is, God: but if thou wilt enter into life, keep the commandments."
>
> Matthew 19:17

The first stipulation to entering into eternal life was to do what God said to do or to follow the commandments, which are God's moral principles that guide human conduct. The young ruler confidently declared that he had faithfully observed these commandments since his youth. However, Jesus could see the barrier that hindered this man from fully embracing eternal life. It was his attachment to his earthly treasure.

> "He that trusteth in his riches shall fall: but the righteous shall flourish as a branch."
>
> Proverbs 11:18

> "And he said unto them, Take heed, and beware of covetousness: for a man's life consisteth not in the abundance of the things which he possesseth."
>
> Luke 12:15

Jesus didn't answer out of indignation or frustration but was moved with love when He looked at the young ruler, challenging him to go beyond the commandments and give up his earthly possessions. He knew the young man's wealth had become a stumbling block, preventing him from fully surrendering to God's will. Jesus spoke of the difficulty for a rich man to enter the kingdom of heaven, using the analogy of a camel passing through the Needle's Eye. It was not merely about relinquishing material possessions but about unburdening oneself from the love of money and pursuing earthly treasures.

> "But they that will be rich fall into temptation and a snare, and into many foolish and hurtful lusts, which drown men in destruction and perdition.
>
> 1 Timothy 6:9

Sadly, the rich young ruler found himself at a crossroads. He was unwilling to let go, but the weight of his possessions proved too heavy to bear. The thought of giving up his wealth and embracing a life of radical faith was too much for him to handle. He remained "almost unburdened," clinging to his earthly treasure rather than embracing eternal life.

> "Set your affection on things above, not on things on the earth."
>
> Colossians 3:2

This case study shows that true wealth and fulfillment cannot be found in accumulating earthly possessions. It reminds us that our hearts and affections should be set on things above, not on the riches of this world. The love of money and material wealth can entangle us, preventing us from fully experiencing the abundant life that Jesus came to offer.

What are the treasures that captivate your heart? Are we willing to let go of anything that hinders us from wholeheartedly following Jesus? The call to unburden ourselves and seek God above all else is challenging but leads to true freedom and eternal life.

> "Lay not up for yourselves treasures upon earth, where moth and rust doth corrupt, and where thieves break through and steal: But lay up for yourselves treasures in heaven, where neither moth nor rust doth corrupt, and where thieves do not break through nor steal: For where your treasure is, there will your heart be also."
>
> Matthew 6:19-21

This story teaches us not to cling to our earthly possessions and miss out on the everlasting treasure. Instead, embrace the words of Jesus, who promises a hope that goes beyond the grave.

Living an "almost unburdened" life, where we cling tightly to our earthly possessions and treasures, ultimately hinders us from experiencing true fulfillment and eternal life. Jesus warned us about the dangers of placing our trust and affection in material wealth. He challenges us to unburden ourselves from the love of money and instead set our hearts on heavenly treasures.

Lets take a look at why this rich young ruler remained "almost unburdened." Despite his desire for eternal life, he was unable to let go of his attachment to his earthly wealth. We are called to go beyond the commandments and surrender everything to follow Him. I know we often hear that salvation is free, the reality is it will cost you everything. Did you know your love for possessions is a stumbling block, which can prevent you from fully embracing the abundant life that Jesus offered.

> "But they that will be rich fall into temptation and a snare, and into many foolish and hurtful lusts, which drown men in destruction and perdition."
>
> 1 Timothy 6:9

The apostle Paul also warns about the dangers of pursuing riches and material wealth. He cautions that those who desire to be rich often fall into temptation, snare, and destructive lusts that lead to their own ruin. The pursuit of earthly treasures can distract us from the true purpose of life and drown us in a cycle of discontentment and greed.

As human beings, we are created with a natural inclination to worship. This desire to worship is ingrained within us because we are made in the image of God. Thus we were designed to have a deep longing for connection, purpose, and meaning in our lives. Worship is the expression of our reverence, adoration, and devotion towards something or someone that we consider worthy of our praise.

However, when we don't choose to worship God, we often find ourselves worshiping other things or idols. An idol can be anything that takes the place of God in our lives, capturing our affections, and becoming the center of our devotion. It can be money or material possessions, success, power, relationships, even our own desires and ambitions.

This tendency to worship other items or idols stems from the brokenness and fallen nature of humanity. Due to the effects of sin, our hearts are prone to wander and seek fulfillment in things that are temporary and ultimately unsatisfying. Some may even mistakenly believe that these idols can provide them with the fulfillment and purpose we desire, but they always fall short.

> "Thou shalt have no other gods before me. Thou shalt not make unto thee any graven image, or any likeness of any thing that is in heaven above, or that is in the earth beneath, or that is in the water under the earth: Thou shalt not bow down thyself to them, nor serve them: for I the Lord thy God am a jealous God, visiting the iniquity of the fathers upon the children unto the third and fourth generation of them that hate me;"
>
> **Exodus 20:3-5**

> "Who changed the truth of God into a lie, and worshipped and served the creature more than the Creator, who is blessed for ever. Amen."
>
> Romans 1:25

The Bible warns us about the dangers of idolatry. God commands His people not to have any other gods before Him and not to worship idols. He knows that worshiping anything other than Him leads to spiritual emptiness and separation from His presence.

When we choose to worship idols, we are essentially exchanging the truth of who God is for a lie. We are settling for temporary substitutes that can never truly satisfy the deep longing within our souls. Our worship is misplaced, and we miss out on the true fulfillment and purpose that comes from a relationship with God.

However, when we choose to worship God, we align ourselves with our true purpose and find genuine fulfillment. God alone is worthy of our worship and devotion.

So, let us be mindful of our innate desire to worship and ensure that our worship is directed towards the one true God. Allow Him to fill the void within us and guide us into a life of true fulfillment and purpose. Instead, we are called to set our affections on things above, not on the things of this earth (Colossians 3:2). Jesus encourages us to lay up treasures in heaven, where they are secure and eternal, rather than accumulating treasures on earth that are susceptible to decay and theft (Matthew 6:19-21). By unburdening ourselves from the love of money and earthly possessions, we free ourselves to embrace the abundant life and eternal treasures that God has in store for us.

Its self-examination time, consider our hearts and consider the treasures that captivate us. Are we willing to let go of anything that hinders us from wholeheartedly following Jesus? Are we willing to unburden ourselves from the love of money and things to pursue heavenly treasures instead? It is a challenging call, but it leads to true freedom, fulfillment, and the promise of eternal life.

> "But seek ye first the kingdom of God, and his righteousness; and all these things shall be added unto you."
>
> **Matthew 6:33**

I pray that we choose not to live almost unburdened lives but seek first the kingdom of God and His righteousness, knowing that all other things will be added unto us. As children of the Most High God, let us prioritize heavenly treasures over earthly possessions, for where our treasure is, there our hearts will be also.

20

Simon - Almost Humble

In the streets of Jerusalem, a young Pharisee named Simon encountered a man who would change his life forever. Jesus of Nazareth, the renowned teacher and healer, captivated the masses with his insightful teachings and extraordinary miracles. With a sense of curiosity and perhaps a touch of skepticism, Simon found himself in this extraordinary teacher's presence.

> "And one of the Pharisees desired him that he would eat with him. And he went into the Pharisee's house, and sat down to meat."
>
> Luke 7:36

As Jesus entered Simon's house for a meal, the atmosphere grew tense with anticipation. Simon observed the actions of Jesus closely, wondering if this man indeed held the power and wisdom attributed to Him. Simon didn't realize that he was nearing a life-altering opportunity, an encounter that could transform his understanding of the kingdom of heaven.

> "And, behold, a woman in the city, which was a sinner, when she knew that Jesus sat at meat in the Pharisee's house, brought an alabaster box of ointment, And stood at his feet behind him weeping, and began to wash his feet with tears, and did wipe them with the hairs of her head, and kissed his feet, and anointed them with the ointment. Now when the Pharisee which had bidden him saw it, he spake within himself, saying, This man, if he were a prophet, would have known who and what manner of woman this is that toucheth him: for she is a sinner. And Jesus answering said unto him, Simon, I have somewhat to say unto thee. And he saith, Master, say on. There was a certain creditor which had two debtors: the one owed five hundred pence, and the other fifty. And when they had nothing to pay, he frankly forgave them both. Tell me therefore, which of them will love him most? Simon answered and said, I suppose that he, to whom he forgave most. And he said unto him, Thou hast rightly judged. And he turned to the woman, and said unto Simon, Seest thou this woman? I entered into thine house, thou gavest me no water for my feet: but she hath washed my feet with tears, and wiped them with the hairs of her head. Thou gavest me no kiss: but this woman since the time I came in hath not ceased to kiss my feet. My head with oil thou didst not anoint: but this woman hath anointed my feet with ointment. Wherefore I say unto thee, Her sins, which are many, are forgiven; for she loved much: but to whom little is forgiven, the same loveth little. And he said unto her, Thy sins are forgiven. And they that sat at meat with him began to say within

ALMOST | 111

> themselves, Who is this that forgiveth sins also? And he said to the woman, Thy faith hath saved thee; go in peace."
>
> Luke 7:37-50

During the gathering, an unexpected interruption occurred. A woman known for her sinful lifestyle entered the room, bearing an alabaster jar of expensive perfume. Overwhelmed by the presence of Jesus, she began to weep, her tears falling upon his feet. In an act of deep reverence and humility, she used her hair to wipe His feet and anointed them with the fragrant oil.

Simon's inward response to the display of affection towards Jesus revealed his skepticism of his prophetic identity. He questioned whether Jesus could be a prophet since, in his view, a genuine prophet should have known the nature of the woman touching him and recognized her as a sinner. This doubt reflects Simon's preconceived notions about what a prophet should be like suggesting that he had certain expectations that Jesus didn't meet. Simon held himself in high regard morally and spiritually, which hindered his ability to grasp the depth of Jesus' compassion and the message of forgiveness he was preaching. Instead of recognizing the grace in his actions, Simon focused on outward appearances and societal norms.

Unbeknownst to Simon, Jesus knew the thoughts of his heart and addressed what was on the young Pharisee's mind. He told a parable of two debtors, highlighting the great forgiveness that comes to those who recognize their need and respond with genuine humility and repentance. In that moment, Simon had a second chance to embrace the kingdom of heaven, to let go of his pride and self-assurance, and to experience the transformative power of grace.

> "Pride goeth before destruction, and an haughty spirit before a fall."
>
> Proverbs 16:18

> "But he giveth more grace. Wherefore he saith, God resisteth the proud, but giveth grace unto the humble."
>
> James 4:6

Simon was almost humble. Outwardly, he portrayed an image of righteousness and devotion, earning the respect of his peers. Yet, deep within his heart, pride lingered, hindering him from fully surrendering to the truth that stood before him. He stood on the threshold of the kingdom of heaven, with something blocking his path.

> "These six things doth the Lord hate: yea, seven are an abomination unto him: A proud look, a lying tongue, and hands that shed innocent blood, An heart that deviseth wicked imaginations, feet that be swift in running to mischief, A false witness that speaketh lies, and he that soweth discord among brethren."
>
> Proverbs 6:16-19

This case study challenges us to examine our own hearts. Are we, like Simon, almost humble? Do we project an image of righteousness while inwardly harboring pride and self-righteousness? The Lord sees and knows our hearts. That means he sees everything like those looks we give that aren't pleasing, those proud looks he hates.

> "The heart is deceitful above all things, and desperately wicked: who can know it?"
>
> **Jeremiah 17:9**

> "Shall not God search this out? for he knoweth the secrets of the heart."
>
> **Psalm 44:21**

> "O Lord, thou hast searched me, and known me. Thou knowest my downsitting and mine uprising, thou understandest my thought afar off."
>
> **Psalm 139:1-2**

Christians have an accountability partner: the comforter, the Holy Ghost. As Jesus helped Simon see that his inward view was wrong, the Holy Ghost also does that for us. Who better to help you than the one who knows everything about you. In reality, it's all about doing what pleases God. The encounter between Jesus and Simon serves as a reminder that genuine humility and openness to God's truth are essential for experiencing the fullness of His grace.

We live in a world where everyone wants to speak their truth at the expense of God. God's Truth matters.

Take this opportunity to reflect upon your life. Are there areas of pride or self-righteousness that hinder spiritual growth? Make a conscious choice not to live an almost humble lifestyle. The posture of your heart matters.

21

Esau - Almost Satisfied

In the land of Canaan, brothers named Esau and Jacob were born to Isaac and Rebekah. Esau, the elder of the two, was a skilled hunter and a man of the outdoors. In contrast, Jacob was a resourceful and clever man who preferred to dwell in tents.

One day, Esau returned from a long hunting trip tired and famished. The smell of food from his brother's pot of stew filled the air, heightening his hunger. In that moment, Esau's desperation grew, and he cried out to Jacob, "Let me eat some of that red stew, for I am famished."

Aware of Esau's weakened state, Jacob saw an opportunity. He replied, "First, sell me your birthright." The birthright granted the firstborn son a double portion of the inheritance and the responsibility for leading the family's spiritual and material affairs.

> "And Jacob sod pottage: and Esau came from the field, and he was faint: And Esau said to Jacob, Feed me, I pray thee, with that same red pottage; for I am faint: therefore was his name called Edom. And Jacob said, Sell me this day thy birthright. And Esau said, Behold, I am at the point to die: and what profit shall this birthright do to me? And Jacob said, Swear to me this day; and he sware unto him: and he sold his birthright unto Jacob. Then Jacob gave Esau bread and pottage of lentils; and he did eat and drink, and rose up, and went his way: thus Esau despised his birthright."
>
> Genesis 25:29-34

Temptation won't last forever; it may be strong but only lasts momentarily. If Esau could speak to you now, he would say, "Don't lose it all for a moment of temptation." In his desperation induced by hunger, Esau disregarded the weight and importance of his birthright. He replied, "Look, I am about to die, so what good is a birthright to me?" Thus, Esau despised his birthright and traded it for a simple bowl of soup.

> "Lest there be any fornicator, or profane person, as Esau, who for one morsel of meat sold his birthright. For ye know how that afterward, when he would have inherited the blessing, he was rejected: for he found no place of repentance, though he sought it carefully with tears."
>
> Hebrews 12:16-17

> "The thoughts of the diligent tend only to plenteousness, but of everyone that is hasty only to want."
>
> **Proverbs 21:5**

Esau's choice to exchange his birthright for a simple meal demonstrated a lack of foresight and an inability to consider the lasting impact of his actions. This shows us how choosing short-term pleasure without thinking about the long-term consequences can be problematic. The important question here is, are we thinking about how valuable the things we give up are? Sometimes, people pressure us into making hasty decisions that don't benefit us in the long run, and we need to be careful about that.

Life presents us with many choices, some of which may appear enticing at the moment but carry enduring consequences. Like Esau's predicament, we are tempted to place immediate gratification above long-term blessings. We need to exercise wisdom and discernment, taking the time to contemplate the ramifications of our decisions acknowledging that our decisions impact not just our own lives but also those of our families and future generations.

In this example, Esau's regret and bitterness stemmed from a hasty choice. It wasn't until much later that he recognized the importance of what he had given up for such a simple thing. Importantly, this isn't unique to Esau; it's something many of us go through as part of the human experience. However, you can avoid this outcome by making wise choices.

This scenario illustrates how we can make choices that initially seem attractive but result in regret. It's like a trap that the enemy sets. Initially, it might provide temporary relief or fulfill a desire, but eventually, you start realizing that something is not right. Over time, you realize the significance of your error, and that sense of regret intensifies.

> "Ponder the path of thy feet, and let all thy ways be established. Turn not to the right hand nor to the left: remove thy foot from evil."
>
> **Proverbs 4:26-27**

> "Wherefore, my beloved brethren, let every man be swift to hear, slow to speak, slow to wrath: For the wrath of man worketh not the righteousness of God."
>
> **James 1:19-20**

> "For which of you, intending to build a tower, sitteth not down first, and counteth the cost, whether he have sufficient to finish it? Lest haply, after he hath laid the foundation and is not able to finish it, all that behold it begin to mock him, Saying, This man began to build and was not able to finish."
>
> **Luke 14:28-30**

> "Without counsel purposes are disappointed: but in the multitude of counsellors they are established."
>
> **Proverbs 15:22**

> "Where no counsel is, the people fall: but in the multitude of counselors there is safety."
>
> **Proverbs 11:14**

The key takeaway here is that not every decision requires hast. It's essential to take your time, carefully consider your options, and weigh the long-term implications before making significant decisions that could affect your life. Also, there are times when you lack complete understanding on a matter. During such times, it's important to seek guidance from trustworthy individuals who offer unbiased advice and have no personal agenda tied to your decision.

> "See then that ye walk circumspectly, not as fools, but as wise, Redeeming the time, because the days are evil."
>
> **Ephesians 5:15-16**

Let's learn from Esau's story and strive to make wise and discerning decisions, considering the long-term impact on ourselves and those who come after us. Value and safeguard the blessings and privileges entrusted to you, avoid letting temporary desires overshadow greater rewards, leaving you almost satisfied.

22

Samson - Almost Disciplined

In the midst of numerous clashes with the Philistines, there resided a man named Samson in the land of Israel. Since birth, he was designated by a divine summons to live as a Nazirite. Endowed with extraordinary strength, a gift bestowed upon him by God, Samson's purpose was to liberate Israel from their oppressors. While some would undertake a Nazirite vow for a brief period, and others for the remainder of their lives, Samson stood apart. His calling was to remain consecrated for the entirety of his days.

> "For, lo, thou shalt conceive, and bear a son; and no razor shall come on his head: for the child shall be a Nazirite unto God from the womb: and he shall begin to deliver Israel out of the hand of the Philistines."
>
> Judges 13:5

Samson was prohibited from consuming wine and other alcoholic beverages, required to avoid anything ceremonially unclean, and most crucially, he was forbidden from cutting his hair, which served as a visible symbol of his devotion to God. The Nazirite vow represented a voluntary act of dedication and sanctification, signifying the individual's desire to draw nearer to God through a period of separation and self-discipline. Despite his strength, Samson struggled with self-restraint. He was driven by his desires and frequently made decisions that compromised his purpose and relationship with God. His struggle with discipline remained a recurring theme throughout his life.

Samson's reliance on his physical strength led him to believe he was invincible to enemy attacks. His judgment was so clouded that he even fell in love with one of his adversaries. Although Samson did not choose to become a Nazirite voluntarily, we can observe how God showed mercy, even when Samson disobeyed his vows. It's important to emphasize that God is not unrighteous. While Samson was disobedient for a time, he was not immediately smitten for his disobedience. It wasn't until he disclosed his secrets to his enemy that he lost his strength. Despite his shortcomings, Samson managed to uphold one aspect of his vow without violation.

See, Samson was disobedient for a while, but it wasn't until he revealed his secrets to his enemy that he lost his strength. Samson had one part of his vow that wasn't violated.

When he told Delilah that his strength came from his uncut hair, symbolizing his vow of dedication to God, she used it against him. As he slept, she cut it off and then began to afflict him, which revealed her true intent. Samson's inside and outside were now in alignment, with his hair missing. She took away the part of his walk with God that he desperately held on to. The Philistines seized him, gouged out his eyes, and imprisoned him. At this moment, Samson faced the consequences of his lack of discipline and the price of disregarding his sacred vow.

But even in his weakened state, Samson's hair began to grow back. The Philistines, in their arrogance, decided to publicly display their captive. They gathered in a temple to mock and celebrate their victory over the once-mighty Samson. The enemy desires to parade you as the one who didn't make it. The one who lived an almost disciplined life. The enemy wants to make sure God can never use you in the same manner again.

I always wondered why Samson lost his strength when his hair was cut, and not for any of his other mistakes. In a passage from the Bible, it says,

> "And the Nazarite shall shave the head of his separation at the door of the tabernacle of the congregation, and shall take the hair of the head of his separation, and put it in the fire which is under the sacrifice of the peace offerings."
>
> Numbers 6:18

Think about it this way: Samson trusted Delilah, who ended up betraying him. In doing so, he revealed his weakness to his enemies, which gave them everything they needed to conquer this conqueror. So, now we see, Samson's loss of strength after his hair was cut was not just about physical hair; it was a symbolic representation of his spiritual and moral downfall due to his betrayal of his vow and trust in Delilah.

As the Philistines celebrated, Samson pleaded with God for one last surge of strength. Positioned between two supporting pillars of the temple, Samson summoned all his remaining strength and pushed against the pillars with all his might. The temple collapsed, killing Samson and all those inside, including the Philistine rulers.

Let's look at what happened. Samson prayed that God would give him the strength to get revenge for his eyes. He was willing to die for his eyes but not to live a life wholly devoted to God. I submit that living for God is more honorable than dying for things. This story helps us to see the importance of discipline and obedience to God's commands. Samson was blessed with incredible physical strength, but his lack of discipline led to a life of compromise and an eventual downfall. He was almost disciplined, but his disobedience and weakness for temptation prevented him from fully embracing his purpose and potential.

> "He that hath no rule over his own spirit is like a city that is broken down, and without walls."
>
> **Proverbs 25:28**

Samson is remembered as a Judge who, for a time, brought deliverance to the children of Israel. Yet this vessel God used to bring salvation needed rescue himself. Samson realized too late that it wasn't his strength that was keeping him. Without discipline, we are like a city with no walls, which means anything can get inside. The fortification and protection come to those who are disciplined.

> "But I keep under my body, and bring it into subjection: lest that by any means, when I have preached to others, I myself should be a castaway."
>
> 1 Corinthians 9:27

This leader of Israel was blinded by the gift of strength that God gave him. They have a saying that I keep hearing, "You are enough!" I'm sure Samson felt the same way. How often do we look at our lives and say, "I am enough!" Friend, let's be honest. All of us have our limitations. Jesus paid the price for our sins because of our imperfections. If we were enough, there would be no need for the sacrifice Jesus made on the cross. In reality, the only one who's ever been enough is Jesus. We can understand our vulnerability to the enemy's attacks when we recognize this and take steps to protect ourselves spiritually. We put on the armor of God, as mentioned in Ephesians 6, to stand firm against the enemy.

In addition to this spiritual armor, we fortify ourselves through prayer, fasting, living a life for God and placing our trust in Him as our ultimate source of strength. Building this spiritual hedge and wearing the armor of God is our way of safeguarding our spiritual well-being and resisting the enemy's schemes.

The more I thought about the story of Samson, the clearer it became to me that everything that happened to him was about who he decided to trust. Samson ended up sharing his deepest, most important secrets with his enemy. This mistake caused a lot of problems for him. It's like when we hear people saying things that make us doubt God. If we pay close attention, we'll notice that these are often the same people who might not have our best interests at heart. It makes you wonder, doesn't it? Who are you sharing your deepest feelings and thoughts with? Do these people genuinely care about what's best for you, especially about your soul? We should be careful not to trust people who would rejoice to see us fail. It's important to share our hearts with those who truly care about us and want the best for us.

> "Casting all your care upon Him; for He careth for you."
>
> 1 Peter 5:7

Samson's story is a powerful lesson about the importance of self-control, staying humble, and keeping our promises. It shows us how bad things can happen when we let our desires and pride control what we do. This story helps us remember that being strong isn't just about how strong our bodies are. Real strength comes from having control over our thoughts and emotions and from being totally committed to following God's. Let's make sure we don't settle for living an almost disciplined life.

23

Gideon - Almost Unwilling

Gideon lived during a time of intense oppression for the Israelites. Despite being perceived by many as unremarkable and hesitant, he possessed humility and found himself in extraordinary circumstances. The Midianites ravaged the land, decimating crops, and pillaging the possessions of the Israelites. This situation prompted the people of Israel to cry out to God for deliverance, yearning for a leader who would emerge and liberate them from their oppressors.

> "And Gideon said unto him, Oh my Lord, if the Lord be with us, why then is all this befallen us? and where be all his miracles which our fathers told us of, saying, Did not the Lord bring us up from Egypt? but now the Lord hath forsaken us, and delivered us into the hands of the Midianites."
>
> Judges 6:13

During the chaos, an angel of the Lord appeared to Gideon while he was hiding, threshing wheat in a winepress. The angel greeted Gideon, saying, "The Lord is with you, mighty warrior." Startled and puzzled by this unexpected greeting, Gideon responded with what sounded like uncertainty. He heard the stories of how the God of Abraham, Isaac, and Jacob delivered His people, but that wasn't what he was seeing. The Israelites had endured this situation for a long time, and Gideon now questioned why God had allowed their suffering and why He had seemingly abandoned them. Little did Gideon know, God would soon answer the questions in his heart.

He received an unexpected message after having the courage to state his frustration.

> "And the Lord looked upon him, and said, Go in this thy might, and thou shalt save Israel from the hand of the Midianites: have not I sent thee?"
>
> **Judges 6:14**

With these words, God unveiled His chosen instrument for deliverance. Gideon's response exposed his uncertain faith and indecisiveness. He questioned his own abilities, citing his low status within his clan. Lacking confidence in himself, he hesitated to embrace the role of a leader and deliverer.

Yet, God knew what He placed in Gideon even though he didn't see it in himself. The Lord recognized the potential within him to be a mighty instrument of His deliverance. And so, He reassured Gideon, promising His presence and guidance throughout the journey.

Gideon, still uncertain, sought a sign from the Lord to confirm His call. He requested that a fleece of wool be soaked with dew while the ground remained dry. When God faithfully granted his request, Gideon asked for another sign, reversing the conditions. Once again, God demonstrated His faithfulness and confirmed His calling for Gideon.

Finally, Gideon embraced his role as a leader and gathered an army of thirty-two thousand men to confront the Midianites. However, God saw that the Israelite army was too large. He understood that the Israelites might boast about their strength in victory instead of acknowledging God's hand at work.

Thus, God commanded Gideon to reduce the size of the army. Gideon obeyed, and the number dwindled to a mere three hundred men. Now, the odds seemed insurmountable, and Gideon faced a crucial decision: to trust in God's promise or to succumb to his indecisiveness and fear.

With his reduced army, Gideon led a strategic attack against the Midianites, armed with trumpets, torches, and empty jars. In the dead of night, they encircled the enemy camp, blew their trumpets, and shattered the pots, creating confusion and panic among the Midianites. The Midianites turned on each other in their confusion, and victory was won by the hand of God. Gideon and his three hundred men triumphed, bringing deliverance to the Israelites and glory to God.

This case study serves as a powerful reminder of the struggles we face when confronted with decisions and uncertainties. Gideon's initial doubts and hesitations resonate with our own moments of insecurity and indecisiveness. At first, Gideon was almost unwilling to step into the role God called him to. However, through Gideon's journey, we learn that God is patient with our doubts and fears. He equips us for the tasks He calls us to, even when we feel inadequate or unsure.

Thankfully, Gideon's initial reluctance didn't last long. He knew he served a God of signs and wonders and asked for a sign, a practice that many have abandoned. Someone desperately needs to know that He is still the same God who answers by fire and performs signs and wonders. When the angel first appeared to Gideon, like many, he sought understanding regarding the suffering around him. However, God's response designated Gideon as the solution for the people. Gideon was not defined by his present identity but by the potential God had placed within him. When God calls us to greater purposes, the adversary often magnifies our weaknesses and past actions. In such moments, we must possess unwavering certainty in embracing what God has declared. Let indecisiveness be definitively cast aside.

I'm not sure what uncertainties you're facing today, but remember that God has called you to be someone's answer. We are called to be the hands and feet of God. Why linger on the fence of uncertainty when you can step into the destiny God has for you? When Gideon embraced his calling, many people were liberated from oppression. When God calls you to something greater, there's no time to hesitate. Remember, God has called you to answer someone's prayer. You don't have to live a life where you struggle, almost unwilling to step into your calling.

24

Simon the Sorcerer - Almost Unchanged

In Samaria, Simon held the city's attention through sorcery. His tricks and enchantments fascinated the people, leaving them in awe of his abilities. However, little did the city know, it was about to undergo a transformation. Philip, one of the early church's deacons, journeyed to Samaria to preach the gospel. His message, filled with conviction and accompanied by miracles, signs, and wonders, led many in Samaria to believe in Jesus. Among those who believed was Simon. Despite his past involvement in witchcraft, Simon was captivated by Philip's message and the miracles he witnessed. As a sign of his newfound faith, he was baptized along with the others who heard the Word of God, though none had yet received the Holy Spirit.

As time went on, it became pretty clear that Simon wasn't all about good intentions. Always curious and after more power, Simon kept a close watch on the apostles, captivated by the incredible things happening around him. Witnessing the powerful effect of the Holy Spirit, he felt a spark of hope, making him reflect on his past choices. He was eager to get that kind of power for himself, to use it like his old magic tricks. He saw how Peter and John laid hands on believers to impart the Holy Spirit. Thinking of what he could do with such power, Simon decided to make a surprising offer. He thought he could simply pay them off and buy the ability to impart the Holy Spirit just like they did. Quite the move, right?

Peter, being perceptive and discerning, saw the darkness lurking beneath Simon's desire for power and rebuked him sharply. "May your money perish with you," Peter declared, exposing the wickedness in Simon's heart. As a new believer, Simon's intentions were impure, but I doubt he knew it, considering witchcraft was what he'd known most his life. Yet this response at root was driven by greed and self-glorification. Peter's words struck Simon like a thunderbolt. The reality of his misguided desires and sinful motives pierced his soul. He realized that he had missed the true essence of the gospel. In a moment of humility, Simon pleaded with Peter to pray for him, acknowledging his darkness and seeking forgiveness.

Let Simon's story serve as a cautionary tale to those who seek to exploit the gifts of the Spirit for personal gain. Simon's greed and desire for control blinded him to the true purpose and meaning of the Holy Spirit. His unchanged mindset led him astray, resulting in dire consequences for his intentions. What made the difference? It was when Peter sharply rebuked Simon for his misguided intentions and informed him that his heart was not right before God. Peter stressed that the gift of the Holy Spirit could neither be bought nor sold, urging Simon to repent for his wickedness and seek forgiveness through prayer.

> "And these signs shall follow them that believe; In my name shall they cast out devils; they shall speak with new tongues; They shall take up serpents; and if they drink any deadly thing, it shall not hurt them; they shall lay hands on the sick, and they shall recover."
>
> **Mark 16:17-18**

This leads us to a question: Do we have faith in God or merely a fascination with what we've witnessed? If the apostles had not intervened, Simon might have become a follower of signs and wonders rather than of Jesus. The Bible tells us that those whom God loves, He corrects. This outward rebuke was a demonstration of God's love for Simon. Simon's request for prayer indicates that he did not possess a stubborn spirit resisting God's correction. Therefore, Simon had an opportunity to repent and avoid remaining unchanged.

Living an Unchanged Life

Leading an untransformed life is similar to burying your talents, as mentioned in the book of Matthew. The Bible warns us against squandering the potential that God gives us. A great danger lies in failing to change, which results in spiritual stagnation and unfulfillment of God's commands. God calls us to develop and utilize our talents for His glory. Misinterpreting Signs and Wonders: Jesus cautioned against seeking after signs.

> "And I was afraid and went and hid thy talent in the earth: lo, there thou hast that is thine. His lord answered and said unto him, Thou wicked and slothful servant, thou knewest that I reap where I sow not, and gather where I have not strawed:"
>
> Matthew 25:25-26

> "But he answered and said unto them, An evil and adulterous generation seeketh after a sign; and there shall no sign be given to it, but the sign of the prophet Jonas:"
>
> Matthew 12:39

Signs and wonders should not be the primary focus of our faith. Instead, our faith should be rooted in a genuine relationship with the Father. Misinterpreting signs and wonders can lead us astray, distracting us from our true values. When we walk in the light as He is in the light, signs and wonders follow those who believe. However, those who believe aren't the only ones who can produce signs. There are some who are of the enemy that also exhibit signs. Remember, everything that God has, the enemy has a counterfeit. Misusing the Gifts of God: In the Bible, we also find guidance on using God's gifts:

> "As every man hath received the gift, even so minister the same one to another, as good stewards of the manifold grace of God."
>
> 1 Peter 4:10

Gifts are entrusted to us as stewards, not for personal gain, but for the betterment of others.

> "For the perfecting of the saints, for the work of the ministry, for the edifying of the body of Christ."
>
> **Ephesians 4:12**

The danger of using these gifts for personal gain is that it causes us to wander from the path of righteousness. God expects us to employ our talents and blessings to serve the world so that He receives the glory, not us.

It's been said over and over, gifts come without repentance. So many gifted people don't follow God, and they glorify the gift instead of the God who gave it. We unpacked a lot in this chapter, but I pray you decide not to live an almost changed life. This is a reminder to all of us to examine our own hearts and motives. Are we seeking spiritual gifts for selfish reasons? Are we desiring power and control instead of humbly submitting to God's will?

The story of Simon urges us to approach the things of the Spirit with sincerity, purity, and a genuine hunger for God's glory rather than our own. I pray this case study helps you to realize that we don't have to remain in a state where we are separated from God. Each day is another opportunity to align ourselves with His will. We don't have to chase after prophecy or a healing ministry just because we see outward signs. The Bible instructs us to know those who labor among us. While many may put on a grand show, it's essential to consider how they live behind closed doors. Follow God, and the signs and wonders will follow you.

25

Gehazi - Almost Aligned

Around the 9th century BCE, a man named Gehazi served alongside Elisha, witnessing firsthand the miraculous acts performed by the power of God. He saw lepers cleansed, the dead brought back to life, and the provision of God in times of scarcity. Yet, in the depths of his heart, Gehazi harbored a dangerous flaw.

> "Now Naaman, captain of the host of the king of Syria, was a great man with his master, and honorable because by him the Lord had given deliverance unto Syria: he was also a mighty man in valor, but he was a leper. And the Syrians had gone out by companies and had brought away captive out of the land of Israel a little maid, and she waited on Naaman's wife. And she said unto her mistress, Would God my lord were with the prophet that is in Samaria! for he would recover him of his leprosy. And one went in, and told his lord, saying, Thus and thus said the maid that is of the land of Israel. And the king of Syria said, Go to, go, and I will send

a letter unto the king of Israel. And he departed and took with him ten talents of silver, and six thousand pieces of gold, and ten changes of raiment. And he brought the letter to the king of Israel, saying, Now when this letter is come unto thee, behold, I have therewith sent Naaman my servant to thee, that thou mayest recover him of his leprosy. And it came to pass, when the king of Israel had read the letter, that he rent his clothes and said, Am I God, to kill and to make alive, that this man doth send unto me to recover a man of his leprosy? wherefore consider, I pray you, and see how he seeketh a quarrel against me. And it was so, when Elisha the man of God had heard that the king of Israel had rent his clothes, that he sent to the king, saying, Wherefore hast thou rent thy clothes? let him come now to me, and he shall know that there is a prophet in Israel. So Naaman came with his horses and with his chariot, and stood at the door of the house of Elisha. And Elisha sent a messenger unto him, saying, Go and wash in Jordan seven times, and thy flesh shall come again to thee, and thou shalt be clean. But Naaman was wroth and went away, and said, Behold, I thought, He will surely come out to me, and stand, and call on the name of the Lord his God, and strike his hand over the place, and recover the leper. Are not Abana and Pharpar, rivers of Damascus, better than all the waters of Israel? may I not wash in them, and be clean? So he turned and went away in a rage. And his servants came near, and spake unto him, and said, My father, if the prophet had bid thee do some great thing, wouldest thou not have done it? how much rather then, when he saith to thee, Wash, and be clean? Then went he down, and dipped himself seven times in Jordan, according to the saying of the man of God: and his flesh came again like unto the flesh of a little child, and he was clean. And he returned to the man of God, he and all his company, and came, and stood before him: and he said, Behold, now I know that there is no God in all the earth, but in Israel: now therefore, I pray thee, take a blessing of thy servant. But he said, As the Lord liveth, before whom I stand, I will receive none. And he urged him to take it; but he refused. And Naaman said, Shall there not then, I pray thee, be given to thy servant two mules' burden of earth? for thy servant will henceforth offer neither burnt offering nor sacrifice unto other gods, but unto the Lord."

2 Kings chapter 5:1-17

Israel and Syria had a complex relationship. Sometimes they fought, and other times, they were at peace, which is why the king of Israel tore his clothes, fearing the Syrian king was seeking an occasion for war. Despite their tumultuous history, the king of Syria showed care for Naaman by sending letters and gifts to Israel. Imagine how much he cared for Naaman to seek help from his enemy. When desperate, you don't care who knows your issues. It wasn't by accident that the young Israelite girl mentioned the prophet in Samaria to her mistress. It was because God desired to heal Naaman. After overcoming some pride issues, Naaman humbled himself and obeyed the prophet. Miraculously, he was healed and offered gifts to Elisha in gratitude. But the prophet refused, knowing that the power of God should never be treated as a commodity.

"But Gehazi, the servant of Elisha the man of God, said, Behold, my master hath spared Naaman this Syrian, in not receiving at his hands that which he brought: but, as the

Lord liveth, I will run after him, and take somewhat of him. So Gehazi followed after Naaman. And when Naaman saw him running after him, he lighted down from the chariot to meet him, and said, Is all well? And he said, All is well. My master hath sent me, saying, Behold, even now there be come to me from mount Ephraim two young men of the sons of the prophets: give them, I pray thee, a talent of silver, and two changes of garments. And Naaman said, Be content, take two talents. And he urged him, and bound two talents of silver in two bags, with two changes of garments, and laid them upon two of his servants; and they bare them before him. And when he came to the tower, he took them from their hand, and bestowed them in the house: and he let the men go, and they departed. But he went in, and stood before his master. And Elisha said unto him, Whence comest thou, Gehazi? And he said, Thy servant went no whither. And he said unto him, Went not mine heart with thee, when the man turned again from his chariot to meet thee? Is it a time to receive money, and to receive garments, and oliveyards, and vineyards, and sheep, and oxen, and menservants, and maidservants? The leprosy therefore of Naaman shall cleave unto thee, and unto thy seed forever. And he went out from his presence a leper as white as snow."

1 Kings 5:20-27

However, Gehazi's heart was enticed by the riches and rewards that Naaman had brought. He secretly pursued Naaman and lied, claiming that Elisha had changed his mind and desired some of the gifts. Unaware of Gehazi's deceit, Naaman gladly gave him the requested items.

But God revealed what he did to Elisha. Gehazi's attempt to profit from the power of God had not gone unnoticed. Elisha confronted Gehazi, pronouncing a severe judgment upon him and his descendants. Due to his greed, Gehazi and his descendants would be afflicted with the leprosy that had been miraculously cleansed from Naaman.

This case study reminds us that God sees everything, even the hidden motives of our hearts. It reminds us that we must walk with integrity and honesty, even when tempted by material gain. Gehazi had witnessed the power of God and experienced His provision, yet he allowed his desire for wealth to cloud his judgment and tarnish his character.

The lesson from Gehazi's story is clear: We must not be content with "almost" walking in alignment. What does it mean to be aligned with God? It means to be wholly committed to righteousness, honesty, and obedience. Good things are not withheld to deprive us but rather to protect us.

> "Now the serpent was more subtle than any beast of the field which the Lord God had made. And he said unto the woman, Yea, hath God said, Ye shall not eat of every tree of the garden?"
>
> **Genesis 3:1**

Selfishness and greed have consequences and pitfalls. Just as in the Garden of Eden, where Adam and Eve were tempted to believe that God was holding something back from them, we, too, can be lured into thinking that God's boundaries and instructions are meant to limit our joy and fulfillment. However, God's guidance is for our good, safeguarding us from harm and leading us to an abundant life in Him.

> "I tell you, Nay: but, except ye repent, ye shall all likewise perish."
>
> Luke 13:3

We often hear stories of people in the Bible who walked down paths where they met with judgment that ended their lives. Why are these examples in the Bible? God wants someone to take heed of His Word. Wisdom is crying out through the scriptures. Will you hear her? Enticed by the love of money, Gehazi gave in to the lust of his flesh. When sin was finished, it brought forth death.

Let's talk about alignment! Having your vehicle's wheels aligned is a necessary maintenance procedure involving all four wheels being correctly positioned relative to each other and the road. Wheel alignment optimizes tire wear, improves vehicle handling and stability, and prevents steering and suspension issues. When your wheels are aligned correctly, your vehicle runs smoothly, you experience less wear and tear, and you have a safer and more comfortable driving experience.

Just as wheel alignment ensures that all components work harmoniously in a vehicle, being "aligned" with God implies that our actions, values, and intentions are in harmony with His will for our lives. In the story, Gehazi fell out of alignment when he allowed the appeal of material gain to misalign his intentions from his values.

This misalignment from honesty and integrity led him to greed and deceit. It's important to know that when you abstain from doing what is righteous, it's replaced with unrighteousness.

> "The heart is deceitful above all things, and desperately wicked: who can know it?"
>
> Jeremiah 17:9

> "For nothing is secret, that shall not be made manifest; neither any thing hid, that shall not be known and come abroad."
>
> Luke 8:17

Even a slight departure from doing the will of God can have significant consequences, just as a minor misalignment in a vehicle's wheels can lead to increased wear and poor performance. We don't know the depths of the deceit hidden within our hearts, but God promised to reveal the secrets within us. Why does he do this? To help us deal with them. It cannot be addressed unless it is brought out into the open.

Now, it's time to examine our lives and assess whether we are "aligned" with God. Are our actions in line with the Word of God? Are we compromising our integrity for short-term gains? Just as wheel alignment preserves the health of a vehicle, aligning our actions with the Most High preserves our character, integrity, and well-being.

Let us pray against living an "almost aligned" life. Let's strive for consistency between our beliefs and actions, like a well-aligned vehicle that smoothly navigates the road. A life in alignment with God doesn't guarantee the road will be smooth, but it means we are prepared for what lies ahead. It prevents us from veering off course and helps us make necessary adjustments to stay on the right path.

26

Eli - Almost Devoted

During Eli's time, the Ark of the Covenant was kept in the Tabernacle at Shiloh. As the high priest and a servant of God, he was to carry out his duties with diligence and reverence. Eli was entrusted with the responsibility of ministering before the Lord and ensuring the spiritual well-being of the people.

> "And these words, which I command thee this day, shall be in thine heart: And thou shalt teach them diligently unto thy children, and shalt talk of them when thou sittest in thine house. and when thou walkest by the way. and when thou liest down. and when thou risest up. And thou shalt bind them for a sign upon thine hand, and they shall be as frontlets between thine eyes. And thou shalt write them upon the posts of thy house, and on thy gates."
>
> Deuteronomy 6:6-9

However, despite his duty to God, Eli neglected an essential aspect of his role: disciplining his children. The law of Moses explicitly commanded parents to train their children in the way they should go. The Law of God was the one thing that should have always been discussed. Eli's sons, Hophni and Phinehas, served as priests alongside their father, but they were corrupt and engaged in detestable practices.

> "Why kick ye at my sacrifice and at mine offering, which I have commanded in my habitation; and honourest thy sons above me, to make yourselves fat with the chiefest of all the offerings of Israel my people? Wherefore the Lord God of Israel saith, I said indeed that thy house, and the house of thy father, should walk before me forever; but now the Lord saith, Be it far from me; for them that honor me I will honor, and they that despise me shall be lightly esteemed."
>
> 1 Samuel 2:29-30

> "Train up a child in the way he should go: and when he is old, he will not depart from it."
>
> Proverbs 22:6

Eli was aware of his sons' wrongdoing, for the news reached his ears and the ears of the people. Yet, he did not take action to correct his sons or hold them accountable for their transgressions. God, in His mercy, granted Eli an opportunity to repent and change the course of his family's destiny. As time passed and he remained unrepentant, God sent Samuel, a young child serving in the temple, to Eli with rebuke and warning. Samuel revealed that because Eli failed to discipline his sons and bring them back to the path of righteousness, judgment would fall on his house. The consequences would be severe, and his descendants would be cut off from serving as priests forever.

> "For I have told him that I will judge his house forever for the iniquity which he knoweth; because his sons made themselves vile, and he restrained them not. And therefore I have sworn unto the house of Eli, that the iniquity of Eli's house shall not be purged with sacrifice nor offering forever."
>
> 1 Samuel 3:13-14

Eli was almost devoted. His negligence in addressing the sins of his own household marred his devotion and led to repercussions. Despite the warning and the opportunity to repent, Eli did not take the necessary steps to rectify the situation and restore righteousness within his family.

> "But if any provide not for his own, and specially for those of his own house, he hath denied the faith, and is worse than an infidel."
>
> 1 Timothy 5:8

> "Therefore to him that knoweth to do good, and doeth it not, to him it is sin." James 4:17

> "Now no chastening for the present seemeth to be joyous, but grievous: nevertheless afterward it yieldeth the peaceable fruit of righteousness unto them which are exercised thereby."
>
> Hebrews 12:11

The story of Eli reminds us of the importance of fulfilling our responsibilities, not only in our service to God but also in our roles as parents or even mentors. It calls us to examine our lives and ask ourselves if there are areas of neglect or compromise that could have lasting consequences. Are we, like Eli, almost devoted? Do we allow sin and wrongdoing to go unchecked in our families? Are we willing to confront difficult situations and make the necessary corrections?

Let's examine these offenses that defiled the house of God:

They disregarded the proper procedures for the offerings brought by the people to God. They would demand their portion of the sacrifices before they were offered on the altar, taking the best cuts. This demonstrated a lack of reverence for the sacredness of the offerings and an abuse of their priestly role.

They engaged in immoral behavior within the Tabernacle. Having relations with women who served at the entrance to the Tent of Meeting showed a disregard for the holiness of God and the sanctity of their roles as priests.

It wasn't just that Eli did not take adequate steps to correct or discipline them as a father, but also as a high priest. His leniency and failure to exercise proper authority contributed to disrespect and irreverence in the house of God.

Lastly, one of the most significant acts of defilement occurred during a battle against the Philistines. Hophni and Phinehas brought the Ark of the Covenant—the symbol of God's presence—onto the battlefield, hoping it would bring them victory. This demonstrated their lack of understanding of the sacredness of the Ark and an attempt to use it for personal gain. The Israelites were defeated in battle, and the Philistines captured the Ark.

This didn't happen overnight but over time. When sin enters our lives, it slowly takes everything until one day you look and the presence of God is nowhere to be found. The Ark, now captured by the Philistines, symbolized God's departure from His sanctuary due to the wickedness and irreverence that had tainted it.

Eli's story reminds us of the importance of respecting the holiness of God, honoring the sacred, and upholding integrity in the service of God. In learning from the mistakes of Eli, we see that it's not acceptable to allow our family to defile the house of God.

Do you remember Hannah? When Eli thought she was drunk, he rebuked her, yet he neglected to reprimand his sons. Something is wrong with that. Friend, don't be content with being almost devoted but strive for wholehearted devotion, knowing that our choices and actions will affect generations. Are there any areas in your life where you are almost devoted?

I'm sure Eli loved his children, yet he was almost devoted. Maybe he didn't want to hurt them. His lack of action in disciplining his children caused his whole family to be removed as priests of God.

The day the Ark was taken, his sons were killed, and his daughter-in-law died during childbirth, giving his grandchild a name that would forever carry a negative connotation: Ichabod. Living an almost devoted life has severe consequences.

> "And she named the child Ichabod, saying, The glory is departed from Israel: because the ark of God was taken, and because of her father in law and her husband. And she said, The glory is departed from Israel: for the ark of God is taken."
>
> 1 Samuel 4:21-20

Reflecting on the story of Eli, we recognize the consequences of living a life that's only partially devoted to God. Many parents have experienced the pain of seeing their children stray from the path of reverence towards God, sometimes leading to tragic outcomes. These situations not only impact the children but also leave a lasting mark on the entire family. The battle for our children's spiritual well-being begins at home. How do we engage in this battle? By guiding them towards the right path, discussing God's teachings whenever possible, and instilling in them a deep respect for God.

However, this message isn't exclusive to parents. While Eli serves as an example, the call for wholehearted devotion to God applies to everyone, regardless of parental status. Devotion to God isn't confined to parenthood. Our faith, our commitment to living according to God's principles, should be a central aspect of our lives, irrespective of our family circumstances. Each of us, by fully committing to God, can positively influence those around us, fostering a community rooted in faith. This involves living out God's teachings in all aspects of our lives, demonstrating that a life devoted to God is not only attainable but also deeply fulfilling and significant.

> "And if it seem evil unto you to serve the Lord, choose you this day whom ye will serve; whether the gods which your fathers served that were on the other side of the flood, or the gods of the Amorites, in whose land ye dwell: but as for me and my house, we will serve the Lord."
>
> **Joshua 24:15**

Despite having knowledge of God, some individuals live an "almost devoted" life. The choice to live this lifestyle can stem from misconceptions about serving God. For some, devotion may seem overly demanding, restrictive, or even morally questionable due to a lack of understanding about God's love and grace. Additionally, external influences from worldly ideologies and societal values can lead to compromises, where individuals prioritize conformity to societal norms over wholehearted dedication to God.

Another thing that holds people back is being scared of what it might cost to fully commit to serving God. Some worry about the sacrifices they'll have to make or the challenges they might face in their personal or social lives if they're totally devoted. This fear leads them to only partly follow God's commands. They end up putting their commitment to God second, thinking more about what they could be missing out on instead.

Lastly, living an "almost devoted" life can come from not growing spiritually and staying in a place where your spiritual journey doesn't go deep. If you don't make an effort to connect more with

God by praying, reading the Bible, and being with other believers, you might find yourself stuck in a comfortable spot, missing out on full devotion. It's crucial not to let fear of committing fully or a wish for an easy life stop you. Make the choice today to move beyond just going through the motions and aim for a life that's completely in line with what God wants. This decision isn't only about avoiding bad things; it's about choosing a way of life that's truly rewarding, one that follows God's guidance and brings a strong and sure faith into not just your life but also positively impacts those around you.

27

Tamar - Almost Mended

Tragedy can strike anywhere, even within the seemingly secure walls of royal households. Tamar, the daughter of King David, experienced this firsthand when she was deceived and betrayed by her brother. No home is exempt when the enemy is seeking whom he may devour. Amnon's malicious intents shattered the life Tamar could have had. It's difficult for me to ask you to imagine her pain, especially considering countless victims have concealed their struggles and cope with experiences like this daily.

So, while I won't go into the details, we can see that when the vile act was done, Tamar lay broken and violated, her purity stolen. Often, victims of rape and sexual assault mourn the loss of their almost life, a life they could have had if not for that situation, now in their minds tarnished forever.

> "And Absalom her brother said unto her, Hath Amnon thy brother been with thee? but hold now thy peace, my sister: he is thy brother; regard not this thing. So Tamar remained desolate in her brother Absalom's house."
>
> 2 Samuel 13:20

The Hebrew word used in this context is "shamem", which has a range of meanings, including "astonished," "appalled," "desolate," "stunned," or "ruined." It conveys a sense of shock, devastation, and emptiness.

"Tamar remained desolate" indicates that she was left in a state of emotional devastation, shock, and emptiness following this traumatic event. The term captures the mental impact of what happened to her.

Although Absalom took matters into his own hands to seek justice for his sister's dignity, Tamar still found herself haunted by the memories of her violation. Revenge cannot erase the scars; even the wrongdoer requires the saving grace of the Lord. While these acts are undoubtedly evil, it's crucial to recognize that everyone needs Jesus.

The deep scars she carried reminded her of the injustices she had endured. Her story is a reminder that in the most esteemed kingdoms, darkness can lurk. Throughout the world, many become victims of rape and molestation. These crimes can impact people from any background regardless of age or sex, leaving scars on their lives. Countless cases remain hidden due to underreporting caused by fear, social stigma, and shame.

Survivors of rape and molestation often face a challenging journey toward healing as they wrestle with the trauma and its aftermath. Tragically, many victims experience decreased self-worth, as if their identity has been robbed by the violations they have endured. This sense of worthlessness, compounded by feelings of isolation and a lack of understanding or support, can lead them to withdraw into silence, feeling unheard and misunderstood in a world that appears indifferent to their suffering.

It's even more devastating when the perpetrators are family members or trusted individuals, as this betrayal further complicates the journey toward recovery. Such a breach of trust ultimately shatters the foundation of trust, leaving survivors feeling abandoned and isolated. In their solitude, they may feel powerless to speak out, convinced that their words hold no weight and will not be acknowledged or validated.

Perhaps, like many others, you have experienced the anguish of losing your innocence and living in a state of being "almost mended." Feeling a range of emotions after such a traumatic experience is normal, and taking the time you need to heal is okay. However, it's crucial not to isolate yourself from the world. While it may be tempting to withdraw and shut yourself off from others, being in the company of friends, family, and caring individuals plays a significant role in the healing process.

You are not defined by the experiences you've faced in life, and your challenges do not diminish your worth. God can heal you from the lingering impact of trauma. While the obstacles we encounter may leave us feeling incomplete, there is hope that we don't have to settle for an "almost mended" life.

God longs to bring healing, restoration, and wholeness into our lives. He offers us the opportunity to be transformed and renewed in Him. Through His presence and divine power, He can mend the fractures we may have encountered along our journey.

> "The Spirit of the Lord GOD is upon me; because the LORD hath anointed me to preach tidings unto the meek; he hath sent me to bind up the brokenhearted to proclaim liberty to captives and opening of prison doors to them that are bound."
>
> Isaiah 61:1

God specializes in healing and restoring all the broken areas within our lives. Through the sacrifice of Jesus, we are granted access to forgiveness, redemption, and the strength to overcome the damage caused by sin and its consequences. The power of God is stronger than any pain or suffering we might have endured. He can mend our wounded hearts, restore our happiness, and bring us to a state of completeness in Him.

It's crucial to keep in mind that healing is a process that takes time and necessitates surrendering our brokenness to God. This involves seeking Him through prayer, studying His teachings in Scripture, and allowing the Holy Spirit to work in our lives. One of the places healing happens is in the presence of God. As we draw nearer to Him, we can encounter healing in His presence.

Also, in drawing closer to God, we can discover hope and strength through our relationship with Him in a world that continues its decline into wickedness. We receive a new identity in Christ, which empowers us to live a life that mirrors His love and righteousness.

> "Come unto me, all ye that labour and are heavy laden, and I will give you rest. Take my yoke upon you, and learn of me; for I am meek and lowly in heart: and ye shall find rest unto your souls. For my yoke is easy, and my burden is light."
>
> Matthew 11:28-30

Dealing with the lingering effects of rape and abuse is difficult when trying to do it alone. Let us not settle for living an "almost mended" existence. Embrace the hope and restoration that God offers us. Permit Him to mend your brokenness and restore your soul.

However, during our healing process, it is absolutely acceptable to seek support from a counselor. There are counselors, including those who specialize in Christian counseling and can provide guidance tailored to your faith. It's crucial not to succumb to the enemy's attempts at getting you to isolate yourself and withdraw from the world because you were created for more and shouldn't have to live an almost mended life.

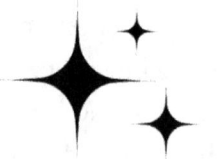

28

Belshazzar - Almost Prudent

In the halls of Babylon, the king, ruler of the mighty Babylonian Empire, held a feast. Despite seeing his father, King Nebuchadnezzar, humbled by the God of Israel, Belshazzar arrogantly ignored the lessons of history. During the celebration, he brought in sacred items from the temple in Jerusalem, which were dedicated to worshiping the true God, and used them to drink wine and praise their idols. This disrespectful act had severe consequences.

> "They drank wine, and praised the gods of gold, and of silver, of brass, of iron, of wood, and of stone. In the same hour came forth fingers of a man's hand, and wrote over against the candlestick upon the plaster of the wall of the king's palace: and the king saw the part of the hand that wrote. Then the king's countenance was changed, and his thoughts troubled

him, so that the joints of his loins were loosed, and his knees smote one against another."

Daniel 5:4-6

"Then was the part of the hand sent from him; and this writing was written. And this is the writing that was written, Mene, Mene, Tekel, Upharsin. This is the interpretation of the thing: Mene; God hath numbered thy kingdom, and finished it. Tekel; Thou art weighed in the balances, and art found wanting. Peres; Thy kingdom is divided, and given to the Medes and Persians."

Daniel 5:24-29

Belshazzar completely missed the mark until the moment the writing appeared on the wall, a clear and undeniable message. It's a bit shocking that sometimes people need such a dramatic sign to realize mocking God is a serious misstep. Many have a habit of brushing aside the wisdom that has been passed down through the generations, almost hitting the target of being prudent, but not quite there. True prudence is about taking the time to think about what your actions might result in and choosing paths that align with what's right and good.

As the hand began writing on the wall, not a single one of his advisors, wise men, or enchanters could make sense of this message from above. At that point, they turned to Daniel, a man of God. The King sought out the man of God, but it was too late for repentance. Daniel clarified that the phrase "Mene, Mene, Tekel, Upharsin" was a dire warning that Belshazzar's rule was judged inadequate and his kingdom was on the brink of being dismantled.

That very night, Daniel's interpretation became reality. Babylon was conquered, and Belshazzar's rule came to a tragic close. Belshazzar's story is a reminder for us to be mindful and deliberate with our choices. It prompts us to think about the ripple effects of our actions. True prudence is when our decisions reflect wisdom and ethical standards, especially in a world filled with distractions and the temptation of instant rewards. In today's quick-paced society, taking a moment to contemplate the long-term consequences of our choices can lead us towards decisions that are not only wise but also just and good.

***Prudence** is a moral and intellectual quality characterized by the exercise of careful and thoughtful judgment in decision-making. It encompasses the ability to consider various factors, weigh potential outcomes, and make choices that reflect wisdom, foresight, and discretion. Prudent individuals often demonstrate a cautious approach to avoid unnecessary risks and act in a manner that aligns with long-term goals, values, and ethical principles. Prudence is not just limited to financial matters but extends to various aspects of life, including personal relationships, business, and ethical dilemmas. It is considered a valuable virtue that promotes responsible and thoughtful behavior.*

Belshazzar's story is a clear example of the consequences of being almost prudent. His hasty decisions and disregard for historical warnings led to his downfall, a scenario we still witness today. He extravagantly wasted resources on his feast, reminiscent of how we can sometimes overspend without saving for the future, creating financial problems. If we don't learn from history, it will repeat itself.

The king's misuse of sacred items for his own celebration reflects today's frequent disregard for spiritual values in pursuit of immediate pleasure, leading to a loss of moral and spiritual direction. We, too, are precious, redeemed at the great cost of Jesus's sacrifice. It's crucial to respect our bodies, the temples of the Holy Ghost, and understand that our actions carry weighty consequences. We ought to steer clear of an almost prudent life, thoroughly evaluating our decisions and seeking wise guidance to avoid unnecessary sorrow. Misusing our bodies through wrongful acts, such as lying, stealing, or fornication, and harboring negative emotions like malice, hatred, envy, and strife, can set us on a path of detrimental habits, addictions, and a sense of emptiness.

> "The simple believeth every word: but the prudent man looketh well to his going."
>
> **Proverbs 14:15**

Every idea that comes into your mind or enters through your ear-gates is not necessarily good ideas. We are called to carefully consider the way we should go. This was an issue for many kings in Israel, so before they would go into battle, many would ask the Lord what they should do. One way to avoid being almost prudent is to inquire what God has to say about it, thus avoiding pitfalls that could potentially cost us our lives. Friend, make up your mind not to live an almost prudent life. So much heartache can be avoided by thinking things through and getting direction from the Lord.

29

The Samarian Woman - Almost Hopeful

In Second Kings, we encounter a sad tale that teaches us the importance of not losing hope, helping us recognize the value of God's gifts, even in the most desperate circumstances.

A City Under Siege

The siege of Samaria, led by King Benhadad of Syria, was a prolonged and burdensome event. The Bible does not specify the duration. Still, it indicates that the siege lasted until a severe famine struck the city, leading us to believe that it endured for a significant period, long enough for the people of Samaria to face the circumstances in this case study.

Typical Events in a Siege

A siege is a military strategy in which an opposing force surrounds a city or fortress, cutting off all supply routes and isolating the inhabitants. This isolation is intended to weaken the city's defenses and force it into submission. The besieging army typically establishes a blockade to prevent food, water, or reinforcements from reaching the city. This tactic is designed to create scarcity and desperation among the residents. As the siege progresses, the people inside the city begin to experience extreme hunger and deprivation. They often suffer tremendously due to limited access to food and other essential supplies.

In some cases, the besieged city may attempt to negotiate a surrender with the besieging force, hoping to secure better terms or end the siege peacefully. These negotiations can vary in their success. In many cases, residents began to lose hope. This battle is in the mind. Distress can lead to extreme measures and drastic actions like the one described in the story from Second Kings 6:24-30, where two mothers contemplated cannibalism out of desperation.

A Mother's Desperation

In Samaria's besieged city, there lived a mother, whose name remains unrecorded in the Bible. Her child, which should have been a symbol of joy and new life, became the center of an agonizing decision when she met another woman, also a resident of the city, both worn down by despair. The woman suggested something horrific, something that challenged their very humanity.

Can you imagine what the people of Samaria went through to reach such depths of hopelessness? Driven to the brink by desperation, she might have considered her baby's feeble cries and the unyielding hunger gnawing at her. Perhaps, in her distorted perspective, she viewed this dreadful choice as a twisted act of mercy, a means to spare her child from the ceaseless agony of starvation.

As I reflect on the decision made and being a mother myself, I can imagine the internal battle this woman faced, torn as the city plunged into darkness under the night's shadow. Perhaps she grappled with the idea that ending her child's life could be misconstrued as a perverse form of love, given the extreme circumstances they were enduring.

The Unthinkable Proposal

I don't believe the woman who approached the mother immediately divulged her plan. Instead, she likely came with a facade of camaraderie, appearing as just another desperate soul trying to survive in the unforgiving conditions of the siege. This initial impression may have disarmed the mother, making her more susceptible to what would come next.

There is no telling how many people she tried this on. She could have engaged the mother in a conversation, gradually steering it toward their dire circumstances and the desperation gripping them all. Strategically planned casual-like behavior allowed her to gauge the mother's emotional state and readiness to consider the unthinkable.

By suggesting that they both partake in this act, the woman conveyed that they were in this dire situation together and had no other options. This illusion of shared responsibility was a manipulative tactic to make the mother feel she wasn't acting alone in her desperation.

By proposing: "cook your son tonight and eat him, and tomorrow, we will cook mine," the woman framed it as an act of kindness, sparing their children from prolonged suffering. Her plan played on the mother's emotions, making her question whether it was more humane to end her child's suffering in this horrific manner. Extreme circumstances can drive individuals to contemplate actions that defy all moral and ethical boundaries.

A Mother's Dilemma

Once the deed was carried out, she was burdened with the consequences of this irreversible choice, which I'm sure gnawed at her heart. Did she convince herself, though twisted in thought, that she was granting her child a merciful escape from the suffering that surrounded them?

The next day, her unease grew. She had anticipated the other woman to uphold their gruesome agreement, to share in the dreadful task they had both reluctantly accepted. However, as the hours passed, the other woman's hesitancy became evident. Panic began to creep into the mother's heart as she realized she had been deceived.

Anger and betrayal overwhelmed her. In her darkest moment, if she truly believed she was acting out of mercy by sparing her child from prolonged agony, this perceived mercy was then snatched away, leaving her more helpless than ever.

Desperate and driven by a sense of injustice, she felt compelled to locate the other woman's child to bring what she deemed as fairness to their twisted agreement. Fueled by feelings of being deceived and manipulated, she couldn't bear the idea of her child being the sole victim of their ordeal. Can you imagine her walking up and down the street, searching for any possible place where the other woman could have hidden her child?

The mother found herself on a grim quest for justice, fueled by anger, betrayal, and desperation. Finally, she cried out to the King, hoping to relieve the darkness within her soul.

> "And it came to pass after this, that Benhadad king of Syria gathered all his host, and went up, and besieged Samaria. And there was a great famine in Samaria: and, behold, they besieged it, until an ass's head was sold for fourscore pieces of silver, and the fourth part of a cab of dove's dung for five pieces of silver. And as the king of Israel was passing by upon the wall, there cried a woman unto him, saying, Help, my lord, O king. And he said, If the Lord do not help thee, whence shall I help thee? out of the barnfloor, or out of the winepress? And the king said unto her, What aileth thee? And she answered, This woman said unto me, Give thy son, that we may eat him to day, and we will eat my son to morrow. So we boiled my son, and did eat him: and I said unto her on the next day, Give thy sun, that we may eat him: and she hath hid her son. And it came to pass, when the king heard the words of the woman, that he rent his clothes; and he passed by upon the wall, and the people looked, and, behold, he had sackcloth within upon his flesh."
>
> 2 Kings 6:24-30

The Lesson

Blinded by circumstances, the mother's actions teach us a profound lesson. Her desperation had cast a shadow so deep that it obscured the true value of what she possessed—her son's life. In that agonizing moment of despair, she had been willing to sacrifice her child, unwittingly failing to recognize that he was more than just a helpless baby; within him was an abundance of potential and future support.

Children hold a position of significance. They are not merely the offspring of their parents but a continuance of their family's lineage and a promise of continuity for generations to come. A child is seen as a gift from God, a blessing to be cherished, nurtured, and protected. They carry with them the hopes and dreams of their parents, a living testament to the family's legacy.

A child held even greater importance for a woman without a husband, like the mother in our story. In a society where family was central to social and economic stability, a child could be the lifeline for a mother with no other means of support. Children were expected to care for their parents in their old age, provide for them when they could not work, and ensure their parents lived with dignity and security. This cultural context adds depth to the mother's desperation, as she faced not only the loss of her child but also the collapse of her future security and well-being.

The mother, in her desperation, had lost sight of all these values. She could not see that her son was not just a mouth to feed but a potential provider, a caretaker, and a source of emotional support in her later years. By sacrificing him, she had unwittingly severed the lifeline that could have sustained her through the trials later in her life, all in the desperate pursuit of immediate relief from hunger.

This case study reminds us of the value of life, even in the most dire of circumstances. Our children are worth preserving, even when desperation threatens to cloud our judgment. In the mother's case in Samaria, her blindness to this truth tragically revealed the depths of human suffering that can result from a failure to see beyond the immediate.

Recognizing God's Gifts

The lesson we can draw from this story is clear: Everything that God gives us is valuable. We must remember that God's gifts are packed with potential when tempted to throw away what we have in our darkest moments.

The story from Second Kings urges us not to be swayed by desperation into making decisions that squander the potential and blessings that God has bestowed upon us. Instead, we should always strive to see the value in God's gifts, even when they might not be immediately apparent.

> "And he said, What hast thou done? the voice of thy brother's blood crieth unto me from the ground. And now art thou cursed from the earth, which hath opened her mouth to receive thy brother's blood from thy hand; When thou tillest the ground, it shall not henceforth yield unto thee her strength; a fugitive and a vagabond shalt thou be in the earth."
>
> Genesis 4:10-12

> "So ye shall not pollute the land wherein ye are: for blood it defileth the land: and the land cannot be cleansed of the blood that is shed therein, but by the blood of him that shed it."
>
> **Numbers 35:33**

In Genesis, when Abel was slain, God said his blood was crying out from the ground. Whenever an innocent person dies, their blood is crying out to God for vengeance. Because Cain killed his brother, the earth would not yield her increase. The land became cursed for the sake of the innocent.

In the book of Numbers, we learn about the cities of refuge. God gives his people a better understanding concerning the shedding of innocent blood. Not only was the land cursed when innocent blood was shed, but the only way to clean the land was with the blood of the one who shed the blood. I'm not saying that if you kill someone, you have to die for it physically. I'm telling you that you have to mortify the deeds of your flesh. When you follow Jesus, the blood he shed atones for your sin. No, it's not automatic. You have to choose him.

We reside in America, a nation known for its freedom, yet the ground bears a curse. If someone were to take a life, typically, there would be an investigation to identify the perpetrator. In most instances, we hope that justice is pursued. We raise our voices against police brutality, but who advocates for the voiceless children who are tragically killed? I'm referring not to those who walk among us, but to the unborn, who also deserve protection and care. The unseen lives in the womb are just as valuable as those we see daily. The enemy seeks to end their lives before they even draw their first breath. It's crucial to be mindful of who we support with our votes, as these decisions impact the protection of innocent lives.

The number of abortions is increasing, and there's a belief that one can terminate a pregnancy even minutes before birth, with people voting in favor of such practices. The argument often centers on "my body, my choice," but what about the mental and emotional toll on individuals dealing with depression stemming from such decisions made in desperation? These studies are often not highlighted, perhaps to avoid acknowledging the consequences.

Whether viewed as population control or child sacrifice, it's crucial for us to recognize the potential in the gift of life that God bestows upon us. While some seek to live without facing consequences, many find themselves in a state of being almost-hopeful, like the Samarian mother we discussed earlier.

Losing hope is like traveling through a storm that won't let up. Some storms are so severe and go on so long that they gradually dim the light in your life. It's like slowly descending into a dark abyss where optimism fades away, leaving an overwhelming sense of despair and disillusionment. Persistent challenges, failures, trauma, or a prolonged sense of helplessness can trigger this decline in hope.

As hope dwindles, so does your sense of identity and purpose. Self-confidence weakens, and clarity about personal goals and aspirations becomes obscured. The once clear path forward becomes muddled, and the ability to define who you are and what you are called to may become elusive.

This despair can lead to a crisis. Where distinguishing between right and wrong becomes challenging. In such situations, many face the difficult decision of whether to keep their unborn child. Medical professionals may not always provide guidance aligned with God's principles.

It's a dangerous thing to choose out of desperation. Desperation clouds your judgment and leads you to choose options that may not be in your best long-term interest. In these moments, it's crucial to try and step back, assess the situation as objectively as possible, and consider the potential consequences of your choices. Remember, it's okay to ask for help and take the time to weigh your options, especially when you're desperate.

Are you currently facing a challenging situation where your hope seems to be fading? When Job experienced a loss of hope, he declared:

> "If a man die, shall he live again? All the days of my appointed time will I wait, Till my change come."
>
> **Job 14:14**

Change might not happen right away. Can you wait for it? If you can find the strength to wait on the Lord, God will help you. The enemy's job is to make it seem like the light at the end of the tunnel has dimmed.

David understood this feeling and penned these words:

> "Why art thou cast down, O my soul? and why art thou disquieted within me? hope thou in God: for I shall yet praise him, who is the health of my countenance, and my God."
>
> **Psalm 42:11**

The Bible also says:

> "Let us hold fast the profession of our faith without wavering; (for he is faithful that promised;)"
>
> **Hebrews 10:23**

> "Which hope we have as an anchor of the soul, both sure and stedfast, and which entereth into that within the veil;"
>
> **Hebrews 6:19**

Never let go of your hope in God. What do I mean by hope? Hope is a confident expectation that good will come to pass. We anticipate it occurring just as God assured us. It is hope that steadies us when our emotions fluctuate. Do you need something to anchor you today? If that anchor is anything other than God, you need something more. This world is seriously lacking; it doesn't fulfill its promises. People may disappoint us, but God can't fail.

In this case study, the mother's worry about her baby consumed her to the point where she forgot her responsibility to protect him.

A siege is intended to manipulate your thoughts. The enemy has laid siege to many minds, causing constant fixation on problems. This cycle of worry can be overwhelming. However, by replacing these concerns with the Word of God and meditating on it day and night, we can gain strength. When the enemy attacks like a flood, the spirit of the Lord will raise a standard against him.

Living a life that's only somewhat hopeful, where you're not entirely sure if things will get better, can also be challenging, even if you aren't overtaken by despair. It's like being stuck between feeling down and having true hope. However, trust that God will help you through tough times. When your hope is anchored in God, no one and nothing can rob you of your joy or peace. Don't settle for an almost hopeful life when you can find true hope in God.

30

Almost Entered In

The Book of Revelation, the last book in the Bible, consists of a series of visions experienced by the apostle John. These visions give insight into the events that will unfold during the last days, often called the "end times." In these glimpses of the future, John witnesses the challenges that humanity will endure. While the 21st chapter mainly focuses on the New Jerusalem, it also tells us who would be excluded from this kingdom. Let's explore these passages in the Bible and their significance:

> "But the fearful, and unbelieving, and the abominable, and murderers, and whoremongers, and sorcerers, and idolaters, and all liars, shall have their part in the lake which burneth with fire and brimstone: which is the second death."
>
> **Revelation 21:8**

This verse begins by highlighting the "fearful" and "unbelieving," emphasizing the importance of faith and trust in God. The "abominable" refers to those who practice detestable and morally corrupt acts. "Murderers" speaks of those who have taken the life of another, while "whoremongers" refers to those who engage in sexual immorality. "Sorcerers" refers to those who practice witchcraft and occult activities, and "idolaters" are those who worship false gods or place other things above God. Finally, "all liars" include people who deceive and speak falsely, even little white lies.

Many say all roads lead to heaven. However, this statement is not accurate. Not every road leads to the same place. As it is in the natural, so it is in the spiritual.

> "Not every one that saith unto me, Lord, Lord, shall enter into the kingdom of heaven; but he that doeth the will of my Father which is in heaven. Many will say to me in that day, Lord, Lord, have we not prophesied in thy name? and in thy name have cast out devils? and in thy name done many wonderful works? And then will I profess unto them, I never knew you: depart from me, ye that work iniquity."
>
> **Matthew 7:21-23**

These descriptions warn us about the sins and lifestyles incompatible with God's righteousness and holiness. When you first start to read this chapter, initially, joy floods in when you think of what God has prepared for those who love Him. Yet, that's it, those who love Him.

> "If ye love me, keep my commandments."
>
> John 14:15

Those who love Him keep His commandments. At the beginning of Revelations, the Bible spoke of the seven churches, saying, "To him that overcometh." This brings to mind the importance of living an overcoming life. I know we are born in sin and shaped in iniquity, but we are called to be holy as He who has called us is Holy, and in another scripture, we are called to perfection.

Friend, If you get anything out of this book, I pray you see the need to allow the Holy Ghost to lead and guide you into all truth. I pray you know the importance of true repentance: deciding to walk in the opposite direction. To leave from giving into lust and pride and follow the God of Heaven. I sincerely pray that you see the need to be transformed by renewing your mind so that you may prove God's good and acceptable will. Many people don't believe it can be done, but you can prove it because "He that is in you" is greater than "he that is in the world."

Let's break that down.

> "Ye are of God, little children, and have overcome them: because greater is he that is in you, than he that is in the world."
>
> 1 John 4:4

> "For all that is in the world, the lust of the flesh, and the lust of the eyes, and the pride of life, is not of the Father, but is of the world."
>
> 1 John 2:16

> "Know ye not that ye are the temple of God, and that the Spirit of God dwelleth in you?"
>
> 1 Corinthians 3:16

Now, we have a better picture of what is being said. When we have the Spirit of God dwelling on the inside of us, then greater is He (the Spirit) that is in us than he that is in the world (Lust of the flesh, The lust of the eyes, and the pride of life.) All sin falls into these categories. Having the Spirit gives us the advantage that we need to overcome.

> "What? know ye not that your body is the temple of the Holy Ghost which is in you, which ye have of God, and ye are not your own? For ye are bought with a price: therefore glorify God in your body, and in your spirit, which are God's."
>
> 1 Corinthians 6:19-20

> "Now the Lord is that Spirit: and where the Spirit of the Lord is, there is liberty."
>
> 2 Corinthians 3:17

> "Hereby know we that we dwell in him, and he in us, because he hath given us of his Spirit."
>
> 1 John 4:13

Some believe you don't need the Spirit to be saved, but John said we dwell in Him because we have His Spirit. Does that mean that everyone with the Spirit is going to heaven? No, many who have received this gift will not enter into the joy of the Lord. Having the Spirit does not secure you a place in heaven; it gives you the power to overcome the enemy. Yet, by having the Spirit, we know we dwell in Him when we obey what He says.

> "I am the true vine, and my Father is the husbandman. Every branch in me that beareth not fruit he taketh away: and every branch that beareth fruit, he purgeth it, that it may bring forth more fruit. Now ye are clean through the word which I have spoken unto you. Abide in me, and I in you. As the branch cannot bear fruit of itself, except it abide in the vine; no more can ye, except ye abide in me. I am the vine, ye are the branches: He that abideth in me, and I in him, the same bringeth forth much fruit: for without me ye can do nothing. If a man abide not in me, he is cast forth as a branch, and is withered; and men gather them, and cast them into the fire, and they are burned. If ye abide in me, and my words abide in you, ye shall ask what ye will, and it shall be done unto you. Herein is my Father glorified, that ye bear much fruit; so shall ye be my disciples. As the Father hath loved me, so have I loved you: continue ye in my love. If ye keep my

> commandments, ye shall abide in my love; even as I have kept my Father's commandments, and abide in his love."
>
> St. John 15:1-10

If we love Him, we will keep His commandments. Salvation isn't something that we can do on our own. We have to abide in him. Our salvation is not one of works but faith. Yet when we have faith, it can be seen by our fruit, which is produced by the works of our faith.

> "Yea, a man may say, Thou hast faith, and I have works: shew me thy faith without thy works, and I will shew thee my faith by my works."
>
> James 2:18

Friend, no one has a monopoly on God; our only claim is that Jesus died for us, and through His sacrifice, our sins can be forgiven. It is through faith in Him that I believe He can keep me from falling. I know I have an advocate with the Father, so if I fall, I can repent and try again. My faith means I will get back up even if I fail. So, although we are saved by grace, the work is believing that He can keep me from falling, and even though I just fell, I choose to get back up. How long do I keep getting back up? Until I get it right. I won't stay in my sin; I'm going to get out of it. After a while, I won't continue to fall for the same things I used to.

> "Now unto him that is able to keep you from falling, and to present you faultless before the presence of his glory with exceeding joy. To the only wise God our Saviour, be glory and majesty, dominion and power, both now and ever. Amen."
>
> Jude 1:24-25

According to the world's standards, you will never be perfect. And that is by design. They show you this unattainable image you can never reach, and then when you consider God, you think it is impossible. Yet, God is the same yesterday, today, and forever more. He does not change. The requirement in the Garden is the requirement that we have today. It wasn't about the tree but obedience.

If we can come to God as little children, willing to be obedient, then perfection is attainable. The intention behind highlighting the sins that will exclude people from the New Jerusalem is not to discourage or condemn but to provide a wake-up call and an invitation to turn away from sin and embrace the truth of the Gospel. God desires that none should perish but that all should come to repentance.

> "The Lord is not slack concerning his promise, as some men count slackness; but is longsuffering to us-ward, not willing that any should perish, but that all should come to repentance."
>
> 2 Peter 3:9

> "And there shall in no wise enter into it any thing that defileth, neither whatsoever worketh abomination, or maketh a lie: but they which are written in the Lamb's book of life."
>
> **Revelation 21:27**

Therefore, the desperate plea to the reader is this: Do not settle for an "almost" faith or an "almost" righteousness. Through Jesus Christ, you can drink from the water of Life freely and have your name in the Lamb's Book of Life. Repent, believe in the Gospel, and allow the power of the Holy Ghost to work in your life.

Jesus spoke about striving to enter God's kingdom and not merely settling for an "almost" entrance. This highlights the need for earnest effort and wholehearted commitment to pursuing a relationship with God.

> "Strive to enter in at the strait gate: for many, I say unto you, will seek to enter in, and shall not be able."
>
> **Luke 13:24**

Striving involves actively working towards a well-defined goal. It requires consistent effort and intentional action. That means it demands commitment, perseverance, and a willingness to overcome obstacles. Striving also requires self-discipline and a mind to push forward. That rules out the fearful and unbelieving. It requires a seeker of wisdom who continues to learn, is prudent, and adapts to the various trials. Unlike something that "just happens," striving is a journey that demands dedication and hard work to achieve your desired outcome.

Jesus uses the imagery of a narrow or "strait gate" to communicate that the path to eternal life is not broad or easy. This restrictive gate means you can't do everything or carry everything you want. It requires an unloading of burdens, which helps you enter free and clear from what is holding you down.

When the Bible says that many will seek to enter but will not be able to, it gives the significance of actively pursuing a relationship with God. One cannot simply have a curiosity or surface-level interest. We must wholeheartedly seek God, placing Him above all else and committing ourselves to obedience and discipleship.

We are called to live a life that honors God and reflects His character. This involves continuously growing in our faith, studying His Word, and seeking His guidance through prayer. It means examining our hearts, repenting from sin, and aligning ourselves with His will. It also includes serving others, sharing the Gospel, and living as ambassadors of Christ in a world that desperately needs His love.

If you've made it to the end of this book, I pray you have made up your mind that you will strive to enter into the kingdom of God. Decide today that you won't settle for almost entering in.

About The Author

I didn't realize the impact that always seeing my mom with a pen and paper to write her thoughts would have on our family until after she passed away. She raised eight writers without pressuring any of us to write. Although I declared that I would never be that person who wrote all the time, just like my mother, it happened. I don't know when it happened, but I am grateful.

My name is Ebony, and I am a writer. It sounds like I'm about to introduce myself as an addict, and in a way, I am. Not that I roam the streets looking for substances to fill a void, but I have this desire to write that I cannot avoid. If I were to suppress it, I fear it would burn like fire, inspiration running through my mind. Then, I have this desire to write my wrongs out for all to see - full transparency. I aim to create content that stimulates the mind, inspiring you to flow, as you grow, and eventually sow into the life of another. Not only am I an author and artist, but I am also a ghostwriter and writing coach who formerly taught storytelling to youth in Baltimore City. "If creative writing were contagious, I'd aim to infect everyone I come in contact with; Education = Duplication."

In 2013, I began assisting youth in Baltimore City to set goals for their future. In an environment where many feel hopeless, my aim is to help someone see that better days are still ahead. I have also guided writers of various ages to become published authors. My experience has taught me that it's not just a lack of experience that prevents individuals from authorship but also personal obstacles like discouragement. I often wonder where I would be if I had allowed discouragement to halt my progress. This contemplation propels me to assist others in setting life goals and narrating their stories. While some require just a nudge in the right direction, others need continuous encouragement, and a few need hands-on guidance throughout their journey. After years of teaching and coaching, I published my first book, "How to Keep Them Reading: A Guide to Writing An Engaging Book," which has now reached a global audience. To God be all the glory!

During the Pandemic, I started Faith2Faith Christian Bookstore, an online Christian bookstore. We also work with authors to help them begin their author business journey. At Faith2Faith Books, "we write like our readers' lives depend on it because it does." With the world headed in the way it is, someone must be willing to stand for what is right. I join the growing number of individuals, unapologetically crying unto the Lord, "Hear am I, send me."

Connect with us:
Website: Faith2Faithbooks.com,
Facebook: Faith2FaithBooks

Other Books By This Author

"How to Keep Them Reading: A Guide to Writing an Engaging Nonfiction Book" - Ebony Lynnel Harris

It's something about words that have the power to attract. With so many new books on the market, how can you keep readers returning? There are so many books on how to write a book. It's easy to get confused as to which one is best for you. In this book, I give readers a proven formula to help individuals write an engaging book. They have a saying, you can lead a horse to water, but you can't make them drink. It can apply to writing. Many authors who start writing don't finish. After building the soon-to-be author up with the knowledge, they need to write their books. We help them find their anchor to hold on to when a difficulty arises, tempting them to throw in the towel. We deal with self-limiting beliefs holding them back from following through, and we talk about the writer positioning themselves for the inspiration that comes to the ready writer. How To Keep Them Reading is an excellent guide to the individual looking to write a nonfiction book that will captivate and engage their audience.

You can find newer books on of Ebony's on www.faith2faithbooks.com

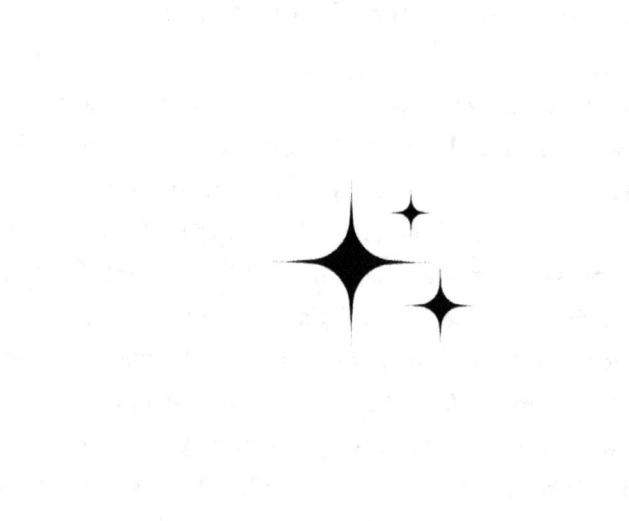

www.ingramcontent.com/pod-product-compliance
Lightning Source LLC
Chambersburg PA
CBHW070058080526
44586CB00013B/1106